VILÉM FLUSSER
THE SURPRISING PHENOMENON OF HUMAN COMMUNICATION

Metaflux 2016

METAFLUX // VILÉM FLUSSER

The Surprising Phenomenon of
Human Communication

1. Communication Theory; 2. Philosophy; 3. Design

First edition ©2016 Metaflux Publishing
Series Editor Rodrigo Maltez Novaes
Art and Design by Chagrin
Published by Metaflux Publishing
www.metafluxpublishing.com

ISBN 978 0 9933272 5 4

Like in so many different ways, I am full of doubts, and short of formed opinions.

V. Flusser, 1975

EDITOR'S NOTE

§ The twelve essays of this book were all written during the second semester of 1975 as Vilém Flusser prepared for a course on the phenomenon of human communication, which was to take place at the *Theatre du Centre* in Aix-en-Provence, France. The course ran from November 6, 1975 to February 2, 1976 and was sponsored by the French Ministry of Culture. At that point, in the mid 1970s, the theory of communication was already a central theme of Flusser's research and writing, and this book falls right in the middle of a series of titles where Flusser started to explore, from a phenomenological perspective, the wider concepts of human communication. However, of all the essay series he produced from this period, *The Surprising Phenomenon of Human Communication* never materialized as a book, despite the individual essays having been printed and distributed in France as part of the deal with the Ministry of Culture. This edition is, therefore, the first ever publication of this title in book format. The lectures were all originally written in both French and English although it is unclear which version he wrote first. Only the last two essays were missing from the English version, so *Alienation and Stereotype* and *Conclusions* were translated from the French versions with the help of Danielle Naves. § In the early 1960s, when he was lecturing on philosophy at the Institute of Technology for Aeronautics, the Polytechnic School of the University of São Paulo, and the Brazilian Institute of Philosophy, amongst other institutions, Flusser began the first production phase of his lifelong philosophical project by working, both directly and indirectly, on the hypothesis of symbolic language as the structure of human reality. § This hypothesis produced all of his main titles of that period: *Lingua e Realidade* (Herder: 1963), *A Influência do Pensamento Existencial na Atualidade* (unpublished: 1964), *Filosofia da Linguagem* (ITA: 1965), *A História do Diabo* (Martins: 1965), *Até a Terceira e Quarta Geração* (unpublished: 1965), *Conceitos Fundamentais do Pensamento Ocidental* (unpublished: 1965), *Da Dúvida* (written in 1965; Relume Dumará:

1999), and *Da Religiosidade* (Cons. Est. De Cultura: 1967). However, when he wrote the essays for *The Surprising Phenomenon of Human Communication*, the working hypothesis that emerged was a progression, development, and mutation from the previous hypothesis of the philosophy of language period; now the structure of communication as the infrastructure of human reality, as well as all of its associated outcomes, became Flusser's new working hypothesis, which he was to explore continuously over the following years until his untimely death in 1991. This second working hypothesis produced all of his main titles on media theory: *La Force du Quotidien* (written in Portuguese in 1971; Ed. Mame: 1973), *Le Monde Codifié* (Institut de L'Environment: 1974), *Natural:Mente* (written in 1974/75; Duas Cidades: 1979), *Gesten* (written in 1976; Bollmann: 1991), *Mutation in Human Relations* (written in 1978; Bollmann: 1996[1]), *Pós-História* (written in 1979; Duas Cidades: 1983), *Für eine Philosophie der Fotographie* (European Photography: 1983), *Ins Universum der Technischen Bilder* (European Photography: 1985),

1. Published in the collection of essays titled *Kommunikologie.*

Vampyroteuthis infernalis (written in 1981; Immatrix: 1987), and *Die Schrift. Hat Schreiben Zukunft?* (Immatrix: 1987). § In 1964 Brazil fell under a military dictatorship that was to last until 1985. The regime's period of highest censorship and repression was during the Presidency of Gen. E. G. Medici from 1969 to '74, due to which, and because of Flusser's earlier life experiences with the Nazis, inevitably resulted in Flusser's desire to leave Brazil. However, during the second half of the 1960s, after a six months trip to Europe and the USA between '66 and '67, where he lectured and met with several philosophers such as Theodor Adorno, Max Bense, and Hannah Arendt, Flusser still continued to lecture in Brazil, although, after publishing *Da Religiosidade*, he did not work on any other book projects until 1971, even so, his literary production did not decrease during this period as he continued to publish essays in several periodicals both in Brazil and abroad. § In 1972 Flusser traveled to Europe to give a series of lectures and to establish contact with different artists and institutions for the following São Paulo

Art Biennial of 1973, with the intention of subsequently returning to his teaching post at FAAP, however, he never returned. Once in Europe he was invited not only to continue lecturing in France, but also to publish again. Shortly after arriving in Europe he published his first two books of his media theory period, after a hiatus since 1967: *La Force du Quotidien* and *Le Monde Codifié*. For Flusser, the 1970s were marked by a significant return to phenomenology, more specifically, to the phenomenology of Husserl and Bachelard. In '73, as he was writing the essays for *Bodenlos*, Flusser writes to Milton Vargas on February 20 about his increased focus on phenomenology, but also on his stylistic experimentations:

§ *...Subjective report: I don't know how to write in French, therefore, I have been writing in English and Portuguese. But the new experiences penetrate none-theless through every pore. I have rediscovered Husserl (and, characteristically therefore, Kant on one side and Ortega y Gasset on the other) in my belly. ... My rediscovery of Husserl is reflected in* As Coisas Que Me Cercam [La Force du Quotidien] *(for example in* [the essay] *"books," which I sent* *to you. Kant, of whom I wrote to you from Megève, is reflected in my methodology, especially the Kant of* [The Critique of] Practical Reason. *And Ortega is once again my stylistic and aesthetic master. (Especially of* On Hunting.*) On revient toujours a son première amour* (sic).

§ And two years later, as he was writing the essays for *Natural:Mente* he wrote to Vargas on February 2, 1975 again commenting not only on his own developing type of phenomenology, but also on his own essayistic style:

§ ...*After you have read the texts, you shall verify the aim: to analyze objects taken to be "natural" by common sense, in order to illuminate, from as many points of view as possible, the problematic of such classifying label. The collection of proposed essays really seeks to be "essayistic": experimental and sketchy. (Essay is a literary form between poetry, philosophy, pamphlet, and journalism, therefore: "post" all of these.) My masters, as you shall verify, are Bachelard and Ortega* [y Gasset]. *However, I take a different path. I seek "to inventory," that is: to open a field for a future disciplined study. In these essays, I am more within the field of a "formalist" tradition and less within the tradition of an existential phenomenology (although strongly nourished by it). And, although less polemic than Bachelard and Ortega, I am, I believe, more engaged. In sum: I am of a different generation.* § In essence, these correspondence excerpts show how objectively Flusser thought about the question of both method and style, which serves to demonstrate, *in nuce*, not only his processual rigour, but also his deep awareness of what he was finally producing. His philosophical project rested firmly upon the concept of philosophical thought as a constantly evolving project, therefore, a philosophy *in fieri*. In order to grasp this further, it is also very important to note that there are fundamentally two chronological lines to be followed when referencing Flusser's books: one that refers to the production dates of the monographs, and another that refers to the publishing dates of these as books. Flusser never interrupted the production flow of his monographs, so that, once a particular monograph was concluded, if he did not already have a publisher interested in the title, he would simply archive the typescript and start on the following monograph. The practice of

writing for at least five hours everyday in the mornings, meant a continuous production flow throughout his life, which at the end, resulted in a typescript archive with more than eleven thousand documents of multiple pages, including monographs, courses, non commissioned essays, correspondence, and papers for symposia. For this reason, it is always important to note the production year of each text, in order to be able to trace the progression of his thought and fundamental concepts. § His thought and ideas were never still, they were in continuous movement, continuously developing, which therefore, means that the monograph production timeline is more valuable in terms of being able to visualise the progress of his ideas. And since Flusser did not date any of his essays, the dating of typescript production can only be done, essentially, through a process of triangulation, using the correspondence of the period, his many own *curricula vitae*, a "forensic" analysis of the typescript by matching the typewriter used and the diagrammatic style of the typescript against the correspondence material, which has dates, and finally, by analysing the very concepts contained in the monograph and their degree of development in relation to the rest of his production. This method invariably produces an accurate date for any typescript in question. However, the correspondence with his closest friends, and especially with Vargas, always produces the most accurate dating. For example, *The Surprising Phenomenon of Human Communication* is the product of Flusser's second phase of intense production, the first one being the mid 1960s. However, this typescript has been incorrectly dated to 1986 in some archive documents, but on November 27, 1975 Flusser wrote to Vargas with a very detailed description of the series of essays he was writing, which leaves no doubt as to its correct date of production:

§ ...*We are now installed for the winter. My course in Aix starts next week. And in Marseilles I shall possibly give another course. Here's the programme for Aix: (1) The surprising phenomenon of human communication. (2) From information to decision. (3) Communication media. (4) The symbolic becoming of man. (5) From scientific discourse to* demagogy. (6) *From family dialogue to the telephone.* (7) *Learning to understand.* (8) *Fashion, from the bible to BB.* (9) *Art: the beautiful and the nice.* (10) *Closed circuits and copying.* (11) *Alienation and stereotype.* (12) *Future Man, will he be a tv-viewer or "a primitive" (third world)?* [2] *The course will be sponsored by the* Ministère de Culture *and the lectures will be printed and distributed. I am already halfway through the preparation of the material, and possibly of seminars to follow each "lecture." But as you know, the idea of giving lectures is very ambivalent for me. I'm a natural teacher, but I am convinced that the discursive lecture is an authoritarian method to communicate no matter what. On the other hand: the dialogic method (for example brain storming and group dynamics) doesn't work yet, as you well pointed out in the case of* "Technologie et Imaginaire." *Like in so many different ways, I am full of doubts and short of formed opinions. ... What also worries me in this sense is the question of the form dialogue has: seminar, committee, symposium, congress, laboratory, forum, parliament, fairs with conversations, epistolary correspondence etc. We shouldn't, I believe, identify dialogue with either "agon" or "eros" (just as we shouldn't identify discourse with authority or fascism), nor should we see in dialogue only the creation*

2. Of this list, Flusser changed the titles of three essays for the final series, namely, numbers four, ten, and twelve, which respectively became *Symbols and Their Meaning*, *The Avant-Garde* and *Closed Circuit Communication*, and *Conclusions*.

of new forms, and in discourse only the transmission of available forms. For example: science is a discourse composed of dialogues, and parliament is a dialogue composed of discourses. Perhaps the difference between the liberal and socialist concept of "democracy," and the difference between the concept of "art" in the so-called avant-garde and mass media, is due to the reigning confusion in relation to the function of dialogue and discourse. Quod dicit magister? And: isn't "history," as a process, "agon" (dialogic), and as testimony, "anecdotal" (discourse)?

§ *The Surprising Phenomenon of Human Communication* is, therefore, an important unpublished title of Flusser's mid career production to finally be published, in the author's own English version, after forty years since it was written.

THE SURPRISING PHENOMENON OF HUMAN COMMUNICATION

§ Contrary to the expression *"zoon politikon,"* Man is not fundamentally a social being. He is, in fact, the most solitary of all animals, even more so than an eagle high up in the sky, or an octopus deep down in the oceanic abysses. He is the most solitary of all animals, even if he lives amidst the demographic explosion which is about to transform humanity into a sort of mobile moss covering the continents: and he is the most solitary of all animals, even if he is in love (which is the most powerful of all types of communication). The fundamental reason for his solitude is the knowledge of his own death; of the fact that he is irrevocably walking towards a situation, which he will have to face alone, for himself, and in which society, with all its artifices called "culture," will become useless and worthless. This absolute solitude in death is, in Man, an ever-present knowledge, and it accompanies, *sotto voce*, his every moment. In fact: it may be held (as it was done by some of the Ancients) that it is this knowledge of fundamental solitude in death, which distinguishes Man from all other animals, and should therefore, form the basis for every type of anthropological study. How should the phenomenon of human communication; of the fact that humans exchange information and store it collectively – to a far greater extent and far in excess, to what even the insect societies are capable of – be seen against this background? Man, the most solitary of animals, is committed to the most intense, and also most extensive type of communication. This course of lectures will try to consider some of the aspects of this marvellous, miraculous, or, to put it modestly, surprising dialectic contradiction. § However, the fact that humans do communicate with each other *is* surprising, and not only from an existential point of view. If we come to consider communication formally, if we ask ourselves what happens when we communicate something, to somebody, somehow, we might find that we are asking a question that admits no satisfactory answer. What I mean, of course, is not that we are unable to describe carefully what happens during communication, nor that we cannot explain the process of communication on numerous levels. Most, if not all, humanist disciplines are concerned with just such descriptions and explanations, and the theory of communication is an attempt at generalisation, formalisation, and quantification of those descriptions and explanations. What I mean is the very simple and brutal fact that there is no possible form of communication that can communicate concrete experience to others. Concrete experience is essentially private: it is unique in the sense of being irreversible, irrevocable, and incapable of repetition, because it is my experience, as it happens to me here and now. Formally speaking, it is easy to show that concrete experience cannot be communicated. Every communication involves some type of intersubjective convention, some code agreed upon by those who participate in it. And every intersubjective convention, even the most apparently obvious one, like pointing with one's finger, is "public" in the sense of being general, reversible, revocable, and capable of repetition. Thus, it necessarily falsifies the concrete experience it is meant to communicate. Therefore, strictly and formally speaking, concrete experience cannot be communicated, and loosely speaking, it can be communicated only in a diluted and dubious way. But if this is so, if the publication of private experience is strictly impossible, even through an intense type of communication such as love, or a dense one, such as art, or a clear and refined one, such as science (not to speak of diffuse and disorderly ones, such as spoken language and the language of gestures), it must then be asked: What is communication all about? Because, if it is not about a concrete experience, then, at least in the last analysis, it must be about nothing. The very simple and brutal fact that concrete experience cannot be communicated tends to be forgotten in the face of the surprising phenomenon of human communication, because, as a matter of course (and paradoxically), most of our concrete experiences happen within, through, and thanks to, human communication. § Obviously, it is common sense that not everything can be communicated, and that in our effort to share our experience with others, we become frustrated. To speak with Wittgenstein, — who suffered this limitation of communication more than most, and who thought about it deeper than most — we constantly throw ourselves against the barriers of language, and history is the collection of wounds we suffer as a result. But this rebellion of ours against the limitations of communication (which is perhaps identical to our rebellion against our human condition) may take various forms. In philosophy it poses the problem of the possibility of objective knowledge, not only necessarily in the Kantian sense, but also in the Positivist sense, as in the problem of observational and theoretical statements. In the arts it leads to an effort to invent new means to communicate experiences not articulated so far; to say what has not yet been said; to utter the ineffable. And in religious thought, it may lead to mystical silence, because, if concrete experience cannot be communicated, then nothing worthwhile can be communicated outside such mute and silent *"unio mystica."* And it is

into this great sea of silence that all rivers of
communication must deposit their turbulent
waters. § Even if the limitations of communication may lead to philosophical *skepsis*, to
artistic frustration, and to mystical silence,
still, what is surprising about communication is not that it is limited, but that it is so
incredibly rich despite its limitations. However, despite the fact that we are fundamentally alone, and that no communication can
change this, and despite the fact that we
cannot communicate what is most concrete,
and thus most important to us, we are still,
all of us, profoundly committed to communication, which is what endows meaning to
our lives. We are committed to communication despite what may be called our
"nature" as mortals, and despite what may
be called the "nature" of communication.

Our commitment to communication is
antinatural in several senses of the term,
because communication *is* society, and
society is not natural to the human animal.
Communication is that situation which
causes neuroses and psychoses, and it is
antinatural because communication is cul-

ture, and culture is anti-nature, since it changes nature and fights against it. Communication is antinatural, because it is history, and history is a negation of natural determination, since it is a quest for freedom. But most of all, our commitment to communication is antinatural because the process of human communication is opposed in its very tendency to the process of nature. Nature as a whole is a process that tends towards entropy, towards progressive loss of information and ever-greater chaos. Human communication as a whole tends towards the progressive increase of information, towards increasingly complex organisation. Nature is a process that tends to become ever more "probable" and therefore ever more foreseeable, and human communication is a process that tends to become ever less "probable" and therefore ever more surprising. This is why it is so incredibly rich despite its natural limitations. And this surprising antinatural character of human communication, and of our commitment to it, suggests that the term "communication" is very closely related to the term "spirit," and that the theory of communication might one day become a general theory of what the Germans call ever since Dilthey "*Geisteswissenschaften*" (sciences of the spirit), which explains, by the way, my interest in it. § However, even though our commitment to communication goes against nature (in many different ways), it is, even so (but in a yet different way), the most natural of all human commitments. So natural is it (in this sense) that we may almost speak of it as an "instinct." Our urge to express ourselves towards others, as well as to open ourselves up to the expressions of others, or in other words, our urge to become "emitters" and "receivers," is almost irrepressible. And such urge to actively and passively participate in communication, society, culture, history, and in the increase of information has been called, in some contexts, our "social instinct." Aside from the fact that the word "instinct" is of little help to explain anything, it is important to bear in mind that our "social instinct" is, quite unlike the instinct of truly social animals, an antinatural drive, and that our communication, quite unlike the communication of social animals, is an artificial process. This contradiction may be condensed, by saying that Man is, by his very nature, an antinatural being, and that this fact becomes phenomenal in the surprising form of human communication. § I said above that human communication is a process that increases information, as opposed to what may be called the process of nature. That was a loose and provisional statement, and we shall go into it more carefully in the course of these lectures. There are, of course, processes in nature that tend from simplicity towards complexity, and the realm of biology is a good example. On the other hand, there is, of course, in human communication, that very curious phenomenon of forgetting, of information loss. But even though the negatively entropic development from protozoa towards mammals is impressive, it may be considered to be an epicycle on the general tendency of nature towards disinformation. And, even though in the course of human communication entire civilisations might have been forgotten, there is no doubt that

The Surprising Phenomenon of Human Communication

to communicate is, as a whole, to accumulate information. However, what is so surprising about human communication is not the evident fact that it stores information against time; that it "memorises" individually and collectively, but that it produces new information. Not, in other words, that it conserves information from entropy, but that it "informs," namely impresses new forms upon the world: that it is deliberately and artificially, "creative." However, let us not delve into the question of where new forms come from, otherwise we shall get lost in metaphysical speculations. Let it suffice to say, at this point, that our almost irrepressible urge to participate in communication has to do with its creative aspect.
§ The general tendency of nature is towards entropy, towards the static equilibrium of chaos; towards what has been called "thermic death." The general tendency of human communication is towards complexity, towards ever-new information, which is a tendency that opposes death. And it opposes death not only in this somewhat abstract sense of opposing the second prin-

ciple of thermodynamics. Human communication does so, much more significantly, on an existential level. One who participates in communication participates in the process of creating new forms. And depending on the extent to which one participates in it, one becomes immortal, because forms are what may be called "eternal." Although we shall all die, and shall die alone, by ourselves, and although no amount of communication can change this, still, we shall not die altogether. Depending on the extent to which we have participated in the creative process of communication, we shall somehow live on within it. We shall be preserved in individual and collective memories depending on the extent to which we have contributed new forms to it, which is a way of saying that, in spite of our death, we shall somehow live on within others. Thus, I believe that this is the true motive of our commitment to communication: *to become immortal within others* — because it is a fact that we know we shall die, and yet we cannot, and indeed must not, accept such knowledge. Our rebellion against death (which is our rebellion against

The Surprising Phenomenon of Human Communication

the human condition) has always taken, is taking, and will probably always take the form, the incredibly surprising form, of human communication. *

Vilém Flusser

FROM INFORMATION TO DECISION

§ In its wider sense, communication is any process, through which, two or more systems are connected. The classical example for such a process in physics are the so-called "communicating vessels." In the sense here intended, communication is the process by which two or more persons exchange information. Human communication is a very special kind of communication. For the purpose here intended, and for reasons that will become obvious as this lecture proceeds, I shall use the word "memory" to describe the systems (persons) that are connected in the process of human communication. And I shall define "memory" as any system that stores information. Thus, for the duration of this lecture, humans shall be information stores, just like libraries, museums, and computers, as well as society, which shall be a net that connects such memories through cables to be called "channels." § One way to visualise a type of memory is to cut a tree trunk and look at its cross section. One may see concentric rings, various irregular traces in the wood, and patches of various colours, and those who have a theory of tree trunks may interpret the forms one sees. The rings may come to mean, years; some traces, worms; some patches, rain, and so forth. Therefore, such forms are "information," in the sense of having been impressed upon the tree trunk: "in-formed." The tree trunk is a memory that stores information. For the observer, the information contained in the tree trunk is "present," in the sense that all the rings, patches, and so forth, are simultaneously available to whoever studies them. They are "synchronic." But they were impressed upon the tree trunk in the course of a time that may have lasted for centuries, and each of the forms may have been impressed at a different moment, which means, the tree trunk was informed in a "diachronic" process. Hence, the tree trunk, as a memory, synchronises diachronic information.

§ Memory preserves, "encapsulates," time for the observer, by presenting information from various pasts onto the same level. Memory is a "time capsule." The information, thus stored in the tree trunk against time, is somehow organised, in the sense that it is impressed upon the tree organism. The tree is the "structure" of the memory we observe when looking at a tree trunk section. Therefore, memory stores information against time in specific structures. Trees are one type of memory structure, libraries are another type, and what is called "the mind" is yet another. Society is a net that connects memories of different structures. § Memories are systems of the "game" type. The information stored in them may be considered to be the "repertoire" of a game, in the sense in which chessmen are the repertoire of the game of chess. And the structure in which they are being stored may be considered to be a "game structure," in the sense that the rules of chess, which organise the motions of chessmen, is the structure of the game. If one considers memories thus, one may apply the theory of games to them, as well as quantify them, in the following way: every given memory stores, at any given moment, a specific amount of information. And it does so according to a number of rules specific to it. The sum of possible combinations of a given repertoire upon a given structure, of a given memory, may be called its "competence," in the sense in which the chess game is competent for a specific number of moves of chessmen according to the chess rules. Hence, it becomes possible to compare between memories of quite different types and say, for instance, that tree trunks are less competent memories than computer ones, and that computer memories are less competent than even the least competent human memory. § There are two types of games: open, or closed ones. A game is referred to as closed if any change of the repertoire requires a change in its structure. Chess is an example. If you introduce a new chessman, for instance a camel between the rook and the knight, you will have to change the rules of the game, and thus have a new game. Chess is a closed game, because its competence, although great, is statically given. And a game is referred to as open to the extent to which it can increase its repertoire ("absorb new information") without having to change its structure. French is an example. If you introduce a new word into that game, you will not have to necessarily change its structure, namely, French grammar. French is a relatively open game, since its competence may be increased by introducing new repertoire ("information") into it. Memories are games of the open type, and communication is that process by which the competence of memories increases. Society is a net that connects open games called "memories" and thus increases their competence. Of course, society itself may be considered to be an open game on a different order of size.

§ Closed games cannot communicate with each other: there is no communication between chess and football. Open games may communicate with each other to the extent to which they are open: French and arithmetics may communicate depending on the extent to which they are open. But there are formal limits to the possibility of communication. I shall mention one limit at this point. In order to communicate, the two games must have repertoires that coincide at least in part. If no element of the repertoire is found in both games, there is no communication, because no "channel" may be established between them, and the "channel" consists of elements that both games have in common. The "strategy" of communication as a connection between games is to establish channels, namely those elements that the repertoires of various games have in common. Society is a net, the wires of which consist of elements that the repertoires of a number of memories have in common. This is sometimes called "common sense" or "consensus." § The more the repertoires of two memories coincide, the easier they communicate with each other. And if they coincide totally, they communicate perfectly. In this borderline case, however, their competences remain unchanged by communication. Every information exchanged was already stored in both memories before communication. This is a "redundant" situation. The less the repertoires of two memories coincide, the more difficult the communication between them will be, but the more it will increase the competence of both, because the communication will supply them with new information: with "noise." Communication between identical repertoires is completely redundant, and impossible between totally different ones, because communication is then entirely noisy. Thus, communication and information are the inverse of each other: the better one communicates the less one informs, and the more one informs the more difficult it is to communicate. The strategy of communication is to find an optimum: a maximum of information, within a minimum of redundancy necessary for communication. My competence is greatly increased if I talk with Chinese Red Guards than if I talk with you, but it is more agreeable to talk with you, it takes less effort. The strategy of communication consists in finding a method of communicating with Chinese Red Guards more easily, and with you more informatively (which is what I am trying to do at the moment). § Human memories are open games of a complex order. They store various types of information onto various types of structures. Various competences are thus present within them, which makes it difficult to compare between them. One may be more competent in the game of chess, and another more in the game of French, one more competent in the game of love, another in the game of commerce. And since the various competences stored in the human memories are open games, they overlap and penetrate each other. This is a formal aspect of what is called "freedom of decision." From the point of view of the theory of games, the word "decision" has two meanings. One is the possibility to apply, within a given competence, one combination of moves rather than another, which may be called: the decision to apply a specific strategy within a game. The other is the possibility to apply various competences to the same situation, which may be called: the decision to use various games in problem solving. In a different context, the latter is the one that comes nearer to what is called "an existential decision." Communication is a process that increases specific competences within a memory. By increasing various competences, it increases the parameter of decision, in both its senses. In the first sense it makes decision easier, because it enriches the competence in a given game. In the second, the quasi-existential sense, it makes decision harder, because the choice of available competences becomes wider. This is an aspect of freedom, and I shall not go into it, because the formal approach of this lecture does not seem appropriate to it, merely suggestive. § You will have gained the impression, I am afraid, that this course of lectures will be theoretical in a bad sense, namely, formally barren. When I talk about memory, for instance, I seem to be talking about computers, not about human beings. Please have patience. I know just as much as you do about the numerous connotations of the word "memory," and that some of those connotations have to do with what is most sacred in our Western tradition. I chose memory to describe Man in communication just as much for those connotations, as it was for the cybernetic meaning of the word. Let me conclude this lecture by evoking some of those connotations. § In the Orphic tradition, which is one of the roots of Platonic philosophy, memory is the very

nucleus of Man, through which he is connected with Heaven, his true homeland. The
waters of Forgetfulness (*lethe*) have covered
up the Eternal Ideas which Man contem-
plated in Heaven before being born. However, those Ideas are still in his Memory, and
may be uncovered through Socratic dialectics, thus, Man will see Truth again
(*a-letheia*). In the Jewish tradition, which is at
the roots of Christianity, memory is that
place where the dead live, and if one speaks
of a deceased person, one adds to his name
the words "let his memory be a grace."
Those two traditions, the Orphic and Jewish
ones, are the two main threads that inter-
weave in Western thought, and their dialectic contradictions propel our civilisation.
Therefore, the contradictory concepts of
memory unfold an ever deeper and wider
field of meaning, and have resulted, at
present, in a number of very different disciplines that have memory for a subject. In
Biology "memory" means genetic information and conditioned reflex. In Psychology it
means the subconscious and available information. In History it means prehistoric

remains and available documentation. In Ethnology it means myth and recorded tradition. Hence, all these and other meanings of the word "memory" were meant in this lecture, and not only the cybernetic, computer meaning, which was the one more expressly elaborated during the lecture.

§ To dig into memory, to uncover what has been covered, may be called an "archaeological" endeavour in a wide sense: to advance in the opposite direction of the diachronic process. And such an advance is made possible thanks to the synchronizing, storing character of memory; thanks to its negatively entropic aspect. What this lecture intended to show was the role that communication plays in this negentropic process. By informing memories it renders them ever more competent, and thus ever more apt to make decisions. And in this context it is now possible to speak of freedom. If we keep in mind what the word "memory" implies, we may say that communication is the process that liberates us from the flux of time by making us ever more competent for decisions against time. *

COMMUNICATION MEDIA

§ The world we find ourselves in is composed of objects, which means: obstacles
that stand in our way (*"ob-iectum"* = thrown
against). But there is a curious dialectic to
objects, if one is to consider them from the
point of view of communication. To be
sure: they stand between us and those we
want to reach, therefore, they obstruct communication. The more objects we accumulate, the lonelier we are, because they fence
us in. On the other hand, however, any
object whatsoever may become a means to
reach the other person: a medium for communication. The walls of prison cells are
meant to be, and are in fact, objects that
isolate those who find themselves between
them. But if one taps a codified message
against them they become the communication media of prisons (which shows, of
course, that the medium is not the message).
The other side of the dialectic is that
objects meant to be media may obstruct
communication. The TV set stands as an
obstacle between family members. Thus, the

field of research in which communicologists work, should include all objects. In fact, however, the specialists' interests have so far been focused only upon objects that are meant to be *media*, those who own them, and those who manipulate them: TV, the press, posters, and so forth. Unwittingly, the specialists have become servants to the establishment that manipulates society by manipulating ever more efficiently the obvious and not so obvious communication media. In this course I shall try to avoid this trap, by assuming a somewhat phenomenological attitude with regard to media. Therefore, I shall not begin by classifying them with the usual criteria, into visual, audio, and audio-visual ones, or into mass media and elitist ones, but I shall begin by looking at their structure. § In my last talk I defined memories to be places that store information according to structures, and I defined structure to be the set of rules that orders the elements of a system. Media are channels between memories, and may be considered thus to be pseudopods, which memories extend towards each other. Like

memories, they are structured information. The prison wall, if tapped on, becomes an extension of the prisoner's memory and acquires the structure of one of his competences. Of course, the wall has its own, objective structure, that of stones, which were ordered in a particular way. And that structure will interfere with the one tapped against it. The message received will be structured by the result of this interference (which is the reason why McLuhan said that the medium is the message). Still: the objective wall structure is the obstacle, and the subjective memory structure is the communicative aspect of the message, and we will have to go much more carefully into this problem in the course of these lectures. Here it must suffice to say that media are structured, and that it is possible to classify them in accordance with their structure. And classify them we must, if we are to find our way through their labyrinthine forest.
§ There is no theoretical limit to possible information structures; to the way information may be ordered. Which is of course a challenge to artists and all those who are

committed to communication. But in fact we may distinguish between only three basic structures: the one that orders information as lines, the one that orders it as surfaces, and the one that orders it as bodies. Examples for the first type are spoken language, alphabetically written language, and music. Examples for the second type are maps, pictographically written language, and painting. Examples of the third type are dance, three-dimensional models of molecules, and sculpture. This is of course only a very rough description. Spoken language and music order sounds into lines (sounds are also "bodies": three-dimensional vibrations), and alphabetic writing orders letters into lines (letters are also two-dimensional figures). Dance orders gestures in space, but it does so within the dimension of time, whereas sculpture orders bodies in space in a way that defies time, and which is meant to defy it. Still: as a first approach, these three basic structure types may serve as a means for orientation. § The important difference between these three types of media is in the attitude they demand of the receiver of their messages. Linear media require the receiver to follow the line to get to the message. This may be called the attitude of "reading." Surface media require the receiver to analyse the surface to get to the message. This may be called the attitude of "imagination." Body media require the receiver to move around them and enter them (at least mentally) to get to the message. This may be called the attitude of "participation." But of course, the matter is far more complicated than here suggested, and not only because the three basic structures may be interwoven. The theatre, for instance, is a medium that combines the linear structure of language and music with the body structure of dance, and thus requires both reading and participation, and the cinema is a medium that lights the surface structure of paintings onto the linear structure of the unwinding film tape, and thus requires both imagination and reading. The matter is also far more complicated for a number of more subtle reasons, and those reasons have to do with what might be called the "quality" of the message. From a merely quantitative point of view, three-dimensional media are of course enormously richer than are linear ones, because their structure permits the ordering of a far greater amount of information. Gesturing with one's body would thus seem to be a far better medium of communication than is alphabetic writing, and those who now prefer it (like the hippies) may seem to have made the correct decision, whereas those who dedicated their lives to music would seem silly. Participation would indeed be superior to imagination, and imagination to reading. This is not necessarily true, and we shall discuss the reasons why in the course of these lectures. § The importance of this difference, between the three attitudes mentioned, cannot be exaggerated, because it is a difference in how we receive messages (and of course also in how we emit them), and a basic difference in how we live: we either read, imagine, or participate in the world. However, "reality," which consists of incommunicable experiences, is obviously not read, imagined, or participated in, but is "experienced." Of course, we sometimes read,

sometimes imagine, and sometimes participate in the world; and we combine these
three attitudes, as well as jump from one to
the other without always being conscious of
it. Still: one of the three attitudes always
prevails over the other two in any given
society, because in every society specific
media dominate over others. For instance,
surface media like painting, calligraphic art,
and ideographic writing (which is structurally identical to pictographic writing) dominate Far Eastern society, and the basic attitude of this society is, therefore,
imagination. Body media like dance, masks,
and sculpture dominate African society, and
the basic attitude of this society is, therefore, participation. And linear media like the
alphabet or mathematical notation (which
resulted in historical action and science),
and music (which is the most noble contri-
bution of the West to human communication) dominate Western society, and the
basic attitude of this society is, therefore,
reading. But this is now changing. Surface
media like TV, the cinema, posters, illustrated magazines, and shop windows become

ever more important, and challenge the dominance of traditional linear media; there are also new cybernetic media, like computers, which have a point-like structure, and which despite being very badly understood are also a challenge to traditional linear media. Thus our basic attitude is changing from one of reading into a very problematic type of imagination, and this is an important aspect of what is being called "the crisis of Western Civilisation." In fact, it is this aspect, and not the more obvious ones, which is the true meaning of the term "communication revolution." The revolutionary event is not that our media are becoming ever more widely branched out, ever more efficient, or ever more cosmopolitan, but that they no longer have our traditional, linear, historical, and scientific structure (which should pose a problem for Marxists). The infrastructure of society, and therefore of human life, is shown to be, by such revolution, not of an economic, but of a communicological nature. In fact, life is changing in the Soviet Union more-or-less in the same way it does in America, because both societies are in the grip of the same communication revolution, and because this revolution seems to leave the other one, the economic and political revolution, in somewhat of a shadow. No doubt: there is an economic, political, and social explanation to the communication revolution, as there is a technological explanation to it. Still: the impact of the revolution shows that it is fundamental, and it suggests that the structure of communication is the infrastructure of society; I shall leave the matter at that.

§ I said at the beginning of this talk that any object in our surroundings may serve as a medium for communication. So the problem of the dominance of a specific medium structure in any given society, and of our present communication crisis, must be seen in that context. Every society tends to codify the world predominantly according to one of the three basic structures, and every object, including the very bodies of humans, · thus becomes a carrier of a specifically structured message. As long as the linear medium structure prevailed in Western Civilisation, every single object of the world

carried a linear message, "told a story."
The world was a book to be read, "*natura libellum*," or a kind of symphony ("the harmony of the spheres," or a progressive curve that could be projected into the future). Every single object, this pipe, or yonder that mountain, which could be decodified within a linear structure, was a sort of letter, or cypher of the "history of the codified world." And science was one of the methods for the decodification of the world. In pre-Socratic Greece a different basic structure codified the world; it was then a "*kosmos*" (a sort of cosmetic article), and every single object had to be decodified according to a three-dimensional structure, such as the structure of bodies like jewels (which is the meaning of the word "*kosmos*"). At present, we are about to re-codify the world. We still read objects around us, but they also carry a differently structured message, which can no longer be grasped through reading. The structure of this new medium requires from us a new attitude towards the world, an attitude of imagination. The world and its objects are no longer a text, but a set

of relations or functions, like a map or a painting. "Historical" decodification is no longer adequate to this newly codified world. Post-history is beginning. § Every single object around us is a virtual medium of communication, because the world is within us, just as much as we are within it. Thus the world and its objects, including ourselves, have, to some extent, the structure we impose on them, which is our memory structure. Therefore, the question whether the mathematical structure (characteristic of linear codes) is in the world or imposed upon it by us, is not a good question. For societies with predominantly linear codes, mathematics is indeed the structure of the world, but not for others. And that is the reason why I have not considered, in this lecture, the usual division of media into visual, oral, audible, tactile, and olfactive ones, or into temporal and spatial ones, nor into those of the elite and those of the masses. These distinctions are no doubt very important, and will be considered later in this course of lectures. More important, it seems to me, is their structural classification, which may be felt, I believe, in every single object, be it visual, oral, audible, olfactive, or tactile. But of course, this poses the question of codification, which shall be the subject of our next lecture. *

SYMBOLS AND THEIR MEANINGS

§ The question of convention, of agreement, of common sense and so forth, was central during the Enlightenment, and Rousseau is an example of the way it was raised. The idea was that humans are superficially different, but that a common denominator, namely reason, could be found in each of them, and that this common denominator was the place where conventions between all humans can be established. To state this idea in the terminology of these lectures: a redundancy exists between the repertoires and structures of all human memories, and this redundancy permits communication between all humans. But if we reformulate the idea in these terms, it changes its impact. Therefore, it is no longer reason alone (namely, that human competence structured by logic), which is the ground for convention, and it is no longer the *"raison d'etat"* or the categories of theoretical reason alone, which permit communication, but now any competence whatsoever may fulfill that purpose. In fact: human communication goes on in the multiple levels onto which the various competences overlap, and reasonable conventions are only one, and possibly not the most important one, of those levels. Which means, we are no longer enlightened. We no longer believe that humans are complicated on the surface, but reasonably "clear and distinct" in essence. Today we tend to believe, on the contrary, that what is clear and distinct about humans is their surface, and that the deeper we delve into them, the more complicated they get. And that is why we can no longer explain very well how conventions happen, how codes are established. § No doubt, some of our codes have been established the way Rousseau imagined: around a round table in a sort of legislative convention. The Morse code, diplomatic codes, and to some extent even the alphabetic code, are examples. In Morse code, somebody proposed: "let '...' mean 'S'," and everybody agreed through some kind of implicit voting. But most of our codes were not established in such manner. Take the code of the French language for instance. No single person ever suggested that the word *"tête"* should mean what *"caput"* means in Latin, although somewhere, somebody, must have proposed this in some way, and this proposition must have carried the day at some given moment, somehow. Other French words, of course, like *"psychanalyse,"* were indeed proposed and accepted more or less like Rousseau wanted. Or take Byzantine painting, no one person ever suggested that a background of gold should mean "transcendence," although of course somebody, somewhere, must have begun that convention, and somehow that convention must have been abandoned at some other time. Or take the codes of dreams, through which the subconscious communicates with the conscious mind. To say somebody proposed that sharp pointed objects in a dream should mean "phallus" seems absurd, but still, some kind of convention on this must have been established. If not, how could psychologists read dreams? § The matter becomes even more complicated if we consider that every code demands some previous code in order to become established, simply because, the convention itself must have been a codified message. The proposition "let '...' mean 'S'" is codified, not in Morse, but in English. The hypothetical proposition "let '*tête*' mean '*caput*'" is codified probably neither in French nor in Latin, but in Frankish, and the code of dreams must be based on some even more basic one, which again must be based on some other code, and so forth. Such consideration leads us into the abyss of "*reductio ad infinitum*," and I believe this is what U. Eco means when speaking of "*struttura assente.*" Again: codes interfere with each other, because the various competences within memory interfere with each other. The Greek language interferes in the code of Byzantine painting, and so does the code of Christian ideology, of Roman law, of dreams and so forth, and the code of Byzantine painting itself interferes in numerous others. We are no longer enlightened and must confess that the human capacity for codification is mysterious, and not only because it is so tremendously complex.

§ Codes are systems that order elements according to rules in such a way that the elements come to represent some other objects, and the rules come to represent some relations between objects. The Morse code is a system that orders electrical impulses to represent letters of the alphabet according to rules that represent the relations between letters. The French language is a system that orders sounds to represent things (including ideas representing things) according to rules that represent the relations between things (including the relations between ideas). Elements representing something are called "symbols," and what they represent is called their "meaning." Three short electrical impulses in the Morse code are the symbol for the letter "S," and that letter is the meaning of those impulses. The sum of the meanings of a code may be called its "universe." The Morse code universe is the alphabet, because Morse code represents its letters and the relations between the letters. Chinese ideograms lie outside the Morse code universe. The universe of French is a specific kind of phenomena, because French represents those phenomena and the relations between them. That universe is not the only one, because there are phenomena and relations that French does not represent (that cannot be said in French). The universe of German is very similar to the French universe, but does not coincide: some things and relations can be said in French but not in German, and vice versa. The universe of Mandarin is even more different from the French one, and the universe of Byzantine painting overlaps even less with the universe of the French language. This raises the question of translations, which is of course fundamental for communication. I shall touch upon it only slightly. § If we want to communicate between universes, we must establish codes that represent the codes of those universes. We can do it, because symbols may represent other symbols. Through such "meta-codes" composed of symbols, representing the symbols of the codes that represent the universes, we may indirectly represent various other universes, however, at a price. The universe of a meta-code is of course broader than the universe of the various codes it represents, but the meaning of the symbols of the meta-code is more indirect, or, as one may say, more formal. One may establish a hierarchy in this way, and establish meta-codes of meta-codes, which become ever more formal. The code of physics is a meta-code of various spoken languages, and in this sense the propositions of physics are bridges that serve to translate between French and German, and even Chinese. And the code of symbolic logic is a meta-code of the codes of various sciences, philosophies, and so forth. These examples illustrate the problem of translation. The sentences of physics do communicate between various sentences of French and German, and thus the universe of physics is common to both these universes. But some other sentences of French and German lie outside the universe of physics and still cannot be translated, because the code of physics does not include the entire universe of French and German. And the universe of physics, although represented by a meta-code of French and German, acquires a proper structure and dynamics because the meta-code of physics acquires autonomy from the codes it was meant to unite. Thus, not every sentence of physics may be translated into French or German. And if we were to establish a meta-code of French and Byzantine paintings, this would be shown even more clearly. I shall drop this problem with the remark that the most formal meta-codes of our civilisation are mathematics and symbolic logic, and that it has been shown that these two codes cannot be reduced one upon the other. § Let me attack the problem from a different angle, because symbols do not only pose the question of "distance." To be sure: the hierarchy of symbols, and symbols of symbols, is a matter of "distance." Symbols that represent concrete experiences (and falsify them by representing them) are at the bottom of the hierarchical pyramid, and at its top are highly abstract (namely theoretical) symbols. But symbols pose also the question of how they represent their meaning: the question of code structure. There are two extremes here. On one extreme each symbol may represent a single element of the code's universe, and each element of the universe is represented within the code by a single symbol. This bi-univocal relation between code and universe is called "denotative." The universe of a denotative code is thus clear and distinct. On the other extreme each symbol may represent a whole parameter of elements of the code's universe, and each element of the universe may be represented by a number of symbols. This equivocal relation between code and universe is called "connotative." The universe of a connotative code is thus confused and compact. In fact those two extremes are never to be found in the existing code structures, even though the code of symbolic logic does approach the denotative structure, and the code of dreams the connotative structure. § The problem of translation, if seen thus, is that every code, including every meta-code, must have a structure. Take the code of the French language and its meta-code of physics as an example: French is of course a code with a very mixed structure, some of it denotative and some of it connotative. It is probably more denotative than German (the famous Latin clarity) but still it is far less denotative than is the code of physics. Therefore the universe of physics has a different, far clearer and more distinct structure than has the universe of French; it is far less confused and compact. And therefore French sentences are falsified if rendered in the code of physics, hence "*tradutore-tradittore.*" On the other hand, the structure of the code of Byzantine painting is probably far more connotative than French or German, its universe is far more confused and compact, and any meta-code of these codes (like logical analysis) will necessarily fail in this aspect. There is, of course, the temptation to say that the meaning of denotative codes is relatively clear, and that the one of connotative codes is richer. If we consider the denotative quality of logics, and the connotative quality of lyrical poetry, we are inclined to believe this. But here again, the matter is more complex. Cabbalism is an example for denotation without clarity, and demagogy (including almost all the messages of mass media) an example of connotation with poverty of meaning. Let me, therefore, insist on the mysterious complexity of human communication. § This mystery becomes denser if we direct our attention to the function of symbols. They "represent," which means they substitute something. But they do so only for those who decodify them (know the code they are a part of). If an illiterate sees an "O," he sees a circle left by a chalk on a blackboard. If a Daoist sees it, he sees the symbol of total perfection. A chemist sees the symbol of an atom of oxygen, and a mathematician sees the symbol of zero. So in a sense, the illiterate is the one who sees the thing, whilst all the others try not to see it. And this pretension not to see the thing in order to see a meaning behind it, a meaning that has been put there through codification, is, I believe, characteristically human. Or, in other words: such pretension is our effort to give meaning to the world ("*Sinngebung*") and also our "alienation"; our opposition to the concrete, stupid absurdity, or whatever, of merely being-out-there. We codify things like chalk molecules into symbols, in order to give the world, and ourselves, a meaning. And this is why human communication is negatively entropic. Symbolic communication is a mere pretense, artifice, and not "real," in the sense of what physics means by "real." An "O" is not really a symbol, but chalk on a blackboard. And thus, symbolic communication is not really subject to the second principle of thermodynamics, because since it is not real, it is not really natural; it is artificial; it goes against nature, though not really. Symbolic communication is what gives us the illusion of dignity in the world. *

FROM SCIENTIFIC DISCOURSE
TO DEMAGOGY

§ Communication is that process by which memories are linked through channels. How the memories are linked is the structure of the process. I shall distinguish here between two basic structures. In the first structure messages flow from one memory in the direction of other memories, and I shall call it "discursive structure." In the second structure messages oscillate between memories, and I shall call it "dialogic structure." An example of the first structure is this talk; other examples are books, the press, TV, posters, concerts, art exhibitions, chain stores, the Church hierarchy, and the hierarchy of public administration. An example of the second structure is the discussion that will follow this talk; other examples are parliament, congress, laboratories, the telephone network, making love, dancing, and fighting. In this lecture I shall consider discourse, and I shall reserve the discussion of dialogue for the next lecture. But a few words must be said immediately with regard to how the two structures are related to each other. § There can be no dialogue without discourse, and vice versa, because in dialogue messages are elaborated for discourse, and in discourse messages are distributed for dialogues. Again: discourse is an aspect of dialogue, and dialogue an aspect of discourse. Take philosophy as an example. Every single lecture and book is a discourse that is part of the philosophical dialogue ("we dialogue with the Greeks"), which again is part of the great discourse of human thought, which again is part of that dialogue between humans concerning the meaning of life, which again is part of the discourse of history, and so forth. Still: at certain places and certain moments one structure prevails over another. The Baroque and the *Ancien Régime* are examples of dialogue domination: the ellipse around the Newtonian sun and around the Sun-king, round tables salons for ladies, minuets, and duels. The French revolution (and the American one) brought us the domination of discourse: inflamed oratory, imperialistic expansion, technological and Darwinian progress, goose-step and television. This

predominance of discourse over dialogue
has become so pronounced at present, that
dialogue is in danger of disappearing. When
people say that they are lonely because they
cannot communicate, they mean the impos-
sibility to dialogue, not inexistent communication. Discursive communication is omnipresent. This is why I shall first consider
discourse: it is the danger that we have to
face now. § In discourse one can distinguish
between a sender and a receiver of information. Information stored in the memory of
the sender is transmitted to the memories of
receivers. The purpose of discourse is to
multiply existing information by distributing
it, and thus preserve it all the better against
the entropic action of time: discourse is
conservative. But discourse can be extremely
dynamic. It may, as the discourse of science
does, absorb ever-new information coming
in from a variety of dialogues, and then
distribute such information. In discourse,
conservatives may be progressives. The
dialectic of discourse becomes evident,
when we take into consideration that overar-
ching discourse, which characterises man-

kind and shows that human communication is artificial: *"paideia."* In *paideia* the sender is one generation, and the receiver the next one. *Paideia* is conservative, because it preserves available information. And it is progressive, because it embodies new information coming in from various dialogues within the body of available information to be distributed. However, evidently, not every *paideia* is equally progressive. The *paideia* of African tribes is less open to new information than was Western *paideia* in the recent past. With the predominance of discourse over dialogue (an apparently progressive phenomenon), our *paideia* may become ever less progressive, because less information from dialogues flows into it. Is this post-history approaching? § Currently, we may distinguish between various discourse structures. Here are the most important examples: the pyramid, the tree, the theatre, and the amphitheatre structures. In the pyramid structure the sender emits information to a number of receivers, who transmit it to an ever-growing number of receiver/transmitters. The army is an example. So is the feudal system. In the tree structure the sender emits information to a number of receivers who transmit, each one, part of it to other receivers by including new information concerning that part, in an ever-growing process of branching-out specialisation. The discourse of science is an example. So is technological progress. In the theatre structure the sender emits information to a number of receivers who form a semicircle that permits a dialogue after the reception of the message. The classroom is an example. So is parliamentary discourse. In the amphitheatre structure the sender emits information towards a circular horizon of mutually non-communicating receivers. Demagogy is an example. So is television. These structures may, of course, be variously combined, and there are other structures, which may come up in the course of these lectures. § The reception of the message can be achieved basically through two methods only: either the receivers open themselves to the sender and admit his message, or there is a mechanism that cracks the receivers so the message can be infiltrated. An example of the first method is the opening of the TV box, and for the second method the way the messages of posters penetrate into receivers. But of course the distinction between the two methods is far subtler. What seems to be an opening up may be the result of a previous cracking. It may be shown, in the case of opening TV boxes, that viewers have been previously cracked up through other media and made to open their boxes. There is however one way to distinguish between the two methods more clearly. If there is, in the receiver, a "zero-order belief" [implicit faith] in the message emitted, we are in the presence of the first method, if not, in the presence of the second method. A "zero-order belief" is the amount of openness of a specific game for noise absorption. It is a mathematical concept and cannot be expounded here. But it is relatively easy to verify its absence. If there is no, or insufficient, "zero-order belief," there is an executive at the disposal of the sender to crack up the receiver. Some of those executive apparatus are carefully hidden, to create the illusion of "zero-order belief" in every receiver. And one of the tasks of communicology is to bring those hidden executives into the open. I suggest that the result of that search will be that there is "zero-order belief" only for the messages emitted by scientific discourse at present. All the other discourses dispose of some overt or covert executives. I shall call discourses based on "zero-order beliefs" "authoritarian" discourses, and those applying executive methods, "tyrannical," and I suggest that science is our only authority at present. § Now if what I Just said is true (and there are very strong arguments to sustain it) we are in a curious situation. Our society has been structured, for hundreds of years, by one dominating authoritarian discourse: the Catholic Church. An enormous majority of receivers had "zero-order belief" in the messages of the senders, including the heretics and other dissenters, since "zero-order belief" is not faith, but readiness to admit the message. And this was coherent with the structure of that discourse: its pyramid structure was perfectly suitable for the authoritarian method of transmission. There was an "author" of the message (God) and a hierarchy of transmitters (the clergy and so forth). Later the "zero-order belief" (and not "faith") began to vanish, and the enormous majority of receivers, including the faithful, closed themselves up to the Church's message. The Church became tyrannical (applied executive methods), lost its authority, and simultaneously, society began to be structured by various dialogic forms of communication. In that situation both authority and tyranny (discursive phenomena) were being pushed into the background. § With the French, the American, the Industrial revolutions, and so forth, discourse became again the dominant communication form. And very soon it took ever more efficient and omnipresent technological aspects. However, all of those various discourses that began to stream through society may be shown to be tyrannical (executive) except one: scientific discourse, which is authoritarian, since an enormous majority of receivers hold "zero-order belief" with regard to its messages, and it disposes of no executive. But this is not coherent with the structure of that discourse: the tree structure has no "author," but is propelled by a very specific kind of doubt called "scientific method." We shall go into it later. From the point of view of communication, however, the scientific method is not operative. Science communicates (distributes its messages) through authoritarian methods. This contradiction between the structure of science and its discourse is an external aspect to what is called the "crisis of science." § To summarise this curious situation we are in: society is characterised by the dominance of discursive over dialogic communication, to a point where the function of dialogue is threatened. Mass media have the amphitheatre structure of discourse that precludes dialogue, and the amphitheatre, which is the horizon of their broadcast, is assuming a cosmic dimension. Discourses with theatre structures, like the cinema and the classroom, and which seem to permit the dialogue of preceding discourses, are losing the impact they had during the nineteenth century and the first half of the twentieth century, because mass media amphitheatres are taking over. Discourses with pyramid structures, which have been classically authoritarian, have become just as tyrannical as are the amphitheatric discourses, because the discourse of science has destroyed our "zero-order belief" in them. Thus: State, political party, enterprise, and so forth, have lost their authority, although not their function. And the tree structure of scientific discourse, which is the only authoritative one in our situation, is in contradiction with its function. § Discourses emit available information to various receivers. They permit that public information may become private. The public man who appears on the TV screen becomes an uninvited guest in the private parlour. The public revelation of God in the discourse of the Church becomes a private experience for the receiver. Discourses, by making the public private, are de-politicising. Dialogues, which publish previously private information, have the opposite, politicising effect, and it is in this sense that democracy is dialogic, but totalitarianism, discursive. The present dominance

Vilém Flusser

of discourse over dialogue points at progressive de-politicisation, and totalitarian structures. A totalitarian structure is not necessarily tyrannical, and the Medieval Church proves it. Since the receivers admitted it's messages, it was an authoritarian structure. But in our situation, the totalitarian society of the future will have to be a tyranny, because it cannot be a scientific totalitarianism, the only one that could conceivably have authority at present. Science contradicts tyranny. But although we are heading undoubtedly toward a totalitarian situation (unless something is done to stop the dominance of discourse at the last moment) the totalitarian de-politicisation of tomorrow may not be felt at all to be tyrannical. People will probably be made to accept it through a sophisticated covering up of executive methods. A "zero-zero-order belief" will thus have been manufactured. A demagogic tyranny is not felt to be one. Since science cannot be an authority, other authorities will be demagogically manufactured. The remainder of this course will be concerned with an analysis of this dialectic between

Page 80   science and demagogy that characterises our situation. *

Vilém Flusser

FROM FAMILY DIALOGUE
TO THE TELEPHONE

§ In my last talk I distinguished between
two ways to link memories, between two
communication structures: dialogue and
discourse. And I said that what characterises
dialogue is the message oscillation between
memories, so that to distinguish between
sender and receiver is no longer very useful.
Of course: if you look at a telephone you
will still find that it has two sides, the send-
ing side that you put against your mouth,
and the receiving side that you put against
your ear. But those two sides are welded
together, which is what distinguishes the
telephone from both a microphone and
a radio receiver, which are separated by a
channel. You may say that the telephone is
a microphone and a radio set become one,
or that a microphone and radio set is a
telephone torn asunder. But by saying this,
you will have driven an important point that
characterises our situation: the technology
behind the telephone and the broadcasting
system is very akin, and there is no technological reason why our dialogic systems

should not be as technically advanced, as
are our discursive systems. The reason why
dialogic systems are lagging far behind must
be elsewhere. § The univocal flux of messages in discourse, as I said the last time, is
what makes discursive communication both
traditional and progressive. The oscillation
of messages in dialogue renders dialogic
communication "responsible" in the sense
of permitting immediate responses. Responsibility is not an immediate answer, but
the capacity for immediate answer, and the
accent should be on the word "immediate."
Of course: we may be capable of answering
even the messages of discourse through one
medium or another. One may send letters
to newspaper editors or use the phone to
call TV stations. But in dialogue it is the
medium itself that permits our answer.
Responsibility is this immediateness of our
capacity to answer. This is why discourse
fosters an irresponsible attitude in the
receivers, while dialogue provokes a responsible attitude even during reception (responsibility is, of course, a political attitude; it is
the capacity and readiness for publication).

And this is the reason why dialogic communication has not been technologically developed. Those who pay for technology have no interest to provoke responsible, namely political, answers to the messages that the established power broadcasts.

§ For the Greeks, dialogue and politics were in fact inseparable concepts. The citizen of the Polis lived in a private house (*"oiké"*), where he manufactured products for sale in the marketplace, and behind which there were fields worked by his slaves and women. This was the private "economic" phase of his life, and it was marked by work *"askolia."* But when the work was done and the product was finished, he left the house for the marketplace, the *"agora,"* in order to exchange it. That exchange established the value of the product. And, of course, that product was not only shoes and tables, but also opinions, *"doxai."* The exchange of products, including opinions, on the marketplace was held not to be work, *"askolia,"* but leisure, *"skolé."* The exchange of opinions was called *"dialogein"* (the exchange of words, *"logoi"*). But of course the exchange of products was also

felt to be part of the dialogic life, of *"skolé."*
And this was the "political" life, because not
only did it establish the value of opinions,
"normai," but also, through such values it
permitted to steer the ship of the State,
"kybernein." These three aspects of dialogue
(*"skolé"* = school, *"normai"* = values, and
"kybernein" = to govern) are those that form
not only the political, but also the creative
type of communication: *a school for normative
cybernetics.* § Memories, linked in dialogue,
consist of various competences: that of
shoemaker, potter, philosopher, and soldier.
Those competences are private: stored
within a particular memory. Through dialogue on the market place they become
public, they become competences of the
Republic. Through their exchange they
achieve a value. They become valuable for
the Republic. But what is even more
important: through their being linked to
each other they create an entirely new competence which somehow jumps, or emerges,
in the process. This new competence is not
only the sum of the competences being
exchanged; it is also an overcoming of all

Vilém Flusser

those competences that participate in it: it is a "synthesis," of which the old competences are "theses." Thus, dialogue may lead, if it is successful, to dialectics: to the creation of new forms, to new information. This is indeed what Socrates was doing on the *agora* of Athens, and what all the dialogues in all the marketplaces are attempting to do. And this is also what "democracy" meant for the Greeks and should mean always: a dialogue that not only steers the ship of the State, but also creates new information. And that is why the Greeks thought democracy was supreme *"poiesis"*: creation. § Today, it is characteristic of our situation that we no longer equate poetry with democracy, or politics with creation. That we have come to believe poetry and creation are processes which go on in isolation. This Romantic belief of ours is an aspect, and a result, of the totalitarian predominance of discourse. No doubt: the new information that emerged from dialogue is stored in the memories of its participants, and thus becomes private. It may then be further elaborated by what Plato called, "inner dialogue." And no doubt also: the new information that emerged from dialogue will be later broadcast through discourse. Still: synthesis is the only way by which new forms may be created, there is no creation "*ex nihilo.*" And Synthesis is a dialogic, political, process. Our tragedy, the tragedy of totalitarian massification, is that we are no longer aware of this. § That is because, what there is left of dialogue in our situation, has been pushed by the dominant broadcasting systems into the private sphere, into "*oiké.*" A paradoxical situation, since dialogue is essentially public. What we still have is the dialogue in the sitting room, in closed laboratories, administrative councils, and in the rarefied atmosphere of government decision-making. The family dialogue and the colloquial conversation are caricatures of dialogues: they do not exchange information to create new one, but only play Ping-Pong with the same information common to all participants, which is received through broadcast. Scientific and artistic dialogues indeed create new information, but they are communicated in hermetic codes to which there is difficult access. They have lost their political dimension. And the dialogues of decision-making (and decision-making is of course the political aspect of every true dialogue) have now become secret, secretive, and only "Secretaries of State" participate in it. In fact, we have lost, or are about to lose, every access to true dialogue, and therefore no longer remember what it is all about. We have become irresponsible, incapable of immediate answer to received information. § This catastrophic de-politicisation of ours (including of those now mistakenly called, "politicians"), is alleged to have a technical reason. The argument goes as follows: in small States like Athens everybody can dialogue with everybody else, but this is no longer possible in colossal States like ours. Discourse can be made available to every-body: TV, the press, posters, and shop win-dows are "open" for millions. But dialogue must always be a closed circuit. The market-place shows this. There can be no dialogue, no exchange of products, in a supermarket. The supermarket discourses in the direction of more-or-less passive consumers. But of

course that argument is a lie in the interest
of those who hold the power of decision.
Dialogic networks may be just as open to
millions as are discursive broadcasting systems. The postal and the telephone systems
are here to prove it. And cable access TV
may prove it even more clearly. The fact is
that the holders of power refuse to make
technology available for dialogic communication. And they thus prevent new information from emerging. Their own discourses
thus become ever poorer in information,
ever more demagogic. And as this process
goes on, the only possibility open to the
establishment of dialogues is revolution.
This is indeed catastrophic. § Let us not
underestimate, however, existing dialogic
systems. We can indeed telephone and write
letters to each other, and in fact we do so to
the extent that it could push those systems
to the point of breakdown. The urge to
dialogue is still alive within us. But of
course those systems cannot satisfy us,
because through them we reach each other
by alphabetic and spoken language only: by
linearly codified messages. We get at the

message but we cannot get at the other person. Dialogue is not only to get a message and to reply to it; dialogue is also to recognise oneself in the other. Dialogue is not only a duel of messages, *"polemos"*; dialogue is also the admittance of the other, "Eros." By its very structure, the post office and the telephone system cannot be erotic, only polemic, even if we desperately try to force them into "Eros." They are important, but entirely insufficient. We must try for other dialogic systems. And this is possible both technically and structurally. Technically it is possible to establish non-linear dialogues, and cable access TV is a first example. Structurally it is also possible, if we remember that dialogues are not necessarily circles like the family or the council, but may be networks like the telephone system. § In sum: we must try to imagine surface based (superficial) dialogic networks. The walls in China are an example for such an imagination. So are the walls in 1968 Paris. But of course, they are not very good examples. They are not good technically, or structurally, nor as far as the messages dialogued

there are concerned. We must do far better, if we are to avoid technocratic fascism of right and left, technocratic discursive totalitarianism. And some such possibilities are beginning to appear on the horizon, new techniques like group dynamics and brainstorming, and new structures like the linking of several circles into a network. One of the purposes of this course of lectures is to provoke in you just such an imagination.
§ I have, myself, a model for such a responsible opposition to the demagogy of totalitarian discourse: philosophical dialogue, under a totally new structure. In the past, philosophy was a dialogue that put all discourses in question. Many say that philosophy is dead now, and for very good reasons, since it is a dialogue of linear structure. I imagine, in my fancy, a philosophical dialogue that goes on in media like the cinema, the poster, and, most importantly, on video: a dialogue that is philosophical in the sense of methodically doubting everything, and which is technically and structurally open to everybody. Of course, such a dialogue must elaborate new codes, and this elaboration must again be

dialogued somehow. All this is my private fancy. But there are symptoms that this is not merely a private fancy. Others seem to have similar dreams, and I believe they are the ones who will really bring about a revolution. A revolution in communication, which, I believe, is the only true political revolution. § The future does not seem to be very promising, if one looks at it from the point of view of communication. If present tendencies continue, we shall be all inserted, very shortly, into a cosmic circus of demagogic broadcast, "*Panem et circenses*," where the accent will shift ever more to "*circenses*." But there is hope still for those who believe that humans may recognise themselves in others. The possibility of dialogue has not yet been entirely eliminated. But we have to do something about it. ✳

LEARNING TO UNDERSTAND

§ In this second part of the course on
the phenomena of communication, our
attention will shift from the structure to
the messages of communication. For the
purpose of simplification, we can distinguish between three types of messages that
humans emit and receive towards and from
each other: (a) messages of knowledge, (b)
messages of desires, and (c) messages of
sensations and feelings. If one formalises
these messages (submits them to what is
called in Logics "propositional calculus"),
it would be easy to show how all types of
massages could be reduced to these three
classes. Class (a) messages are indicatives,
class (b) are imperatives, and class (c) are
exclamations. Of course: there are propositions in question form. But it may be shown
that questions ask for answers within one of
the three classes mentioned. This distinction
into three classes of messages is traditional.
Class (a) is "epistemological" and its ideal is
"truth," class (b) is "ethical" and its ideal is
"the good," and class (c) is "aesthetic" and

its ideal is "beauty." The most important type of communication of class (a) is science, of class (b) is politics, and of class (c) is art. But of course this schematic distinction is pure abstraction. Every factual communication is a mixture of all three classes, and, what is more important, each class may assume the appearance of some other class: imperatives may look like indicatives; indicatives like exclamations, and so forth. This mixture and this masquerade are dangerously misleading, and are a powerful weapon for the manipulation of society by mass media. What seems to be "science" or "art" may often be shown to be in reality a masked imperative, which, because it is masked, are better at changing the behavioural patterns of receivers. One of the duties of communicology is precisely to analyse messages in order to unmask them: to de-ideologise them. The present lecture will consider class (a) messages, those concerning knowledge. § A word of caution: although all messages may be formally classified, as proposed here, most messages are "nonsense." Which means that, if formally analysed, they show no information. And it has been calculated that about 80% of human communication is nonsense. In mass media this proportion is probably much greater. And this is especially true where messages about knowledge are concerned. By far, the greatest parts of those messages contain no knowledge, but are pseudo-propositions. This important problem will not be considered here, but in a later lecture. § A message of knowledge, an indicative, is a sentence of the "function" type ("xfy"): it predicates (pre-dicts) a "subject" in function of an "object" within a situation. The whole problem of epistemology, of how we can know, is contained in this simple statement. This is unfortunately not the place to go into the problem. Let it suffice to say that the problem involves "grammar," namely the philosophy of language, and that the philosophy of science ("epistemology" in the strict sense), is a philosophy of the sentences pronounced in scientific discourse. What must be stressed here, however, is the obvious fact that not all messages of knowledge are codified in spoken or written language. Knowledge may be communicated in any code: through images, dance, music, and so forth. The fact that science is at present our most important communication of knowledge, and that science uses linguistic codes, or codes derived from language, makes us often forget this. Therefore, if I said that a message of knowledge is a sentence of the "function" type, the term "sentence" did not mean a set of words only, and if I said that the problem of epistemology is linguistic, then I meant "linguistic" in all possible codes (not *"langue,"* but *"langage"*). Still: spoken language, and more especially the type of language spoken in the West (the "subject/predicate" language) is the obvious model for our analyses of all messages of knowledge. § This is so, because there can be no question about the fact that science is our model of knowledge, and that science is codified by codes which have the fundamental structure of "subject/ predicate" languages. In this sense, science is profoundly Western. Languages that do not have this structure, like some agglutinative languages of Africa and America, or some isolating languages of the Far East, communicate a different sort of knowledge. Our difficulty is that we may perhaps learn to understand this sort of knowledge through imagination and participation (through our two- and three-dimensional codes), but not through linear, logical reading. And since our model of knowledge is science, this sort of knowledge must remain on the periphery for us, despite our efforts to incorporate it into our memories (see: how African and Mexican magic, Daoism, and Zen Buddhism are being experimented with in the USA and in Europe). § Our memories are structured, at present, by a "zero-order belief" in scientific messages of knowledge, and we are competent to receive such messages (to "understand them") in their "subject/pred-icate" structure. Of course we have other competences as well. If we contemplate a work of art, a cathedral, or a symphony, we may gain knowledge; understand such an indicative message, although it is of an entirely different structure. And we know that such a message is different from the aesthetic message that comes from the work of art, although closely related to it. Art does reveal "truth" for us. Still: for us, it is in the "subject/predicate" structure, this very specific sort of function, where the model of all knowledge is to be found. To know, for us, is to understand that "A is B," because this is how our memories have been programmed. In the end, we reduce every other type of function to this one. Very much like a computer. § This structure suggests how we receive messages concerning knowledge, how we "learn" (if by "learning" we mean acquiring knowledge, which is a restrictive use of that term). A message comes to our memory through some channel, and if we know the code, we decodify it. The message then shows to be an indicative, a message concerning knowledge. If it has the same structure as our competence, we can absorb it, if not, we do not understand it. After having absorbed it, we compare it with other such messages already stored in our memory. If it fits into them, it can be stored, and is taken as "true." If it does not fit, we may either re-arrange the messages already stored, and thus make room for the new message. In this case we have changed

our knowledge, and to be "true" is a different criterion before and after the reception
of this message. Or we may not be able to
re-arrange the messages already stored, and
then the new message cannot be stored. So it
is then taken as "false." Thus, the process of
learning, of acquiring new knowledge, goes
on upon several levels: of code, memory
structure, and repertoire contained in that
structure. I shall consider the problems
posed by the code level in a future lecture,
but I draw your attention to what I have
already said when considering the problem
of translation. Here I shall discuss very
rapidly the problems on the structural and
repertoire levels only, because they have
become very pressing at present.

§ The storing capacity of human memories
is limited, although very great. It may be
true that we do not utilise the entire storing
capacity of our brain, but there must be
good reasons why we do not do it. On the
other hand, the amount of available messages of knowledge has become enormous,
and is increasing with every moment that
passes. This is due to the tree structure

of scientific discourse. We are rapidly approaching a point where it is no longer possible to store such messages in our memory; in fact we may have already passed such point. This is what is imprecisely known as the "inflation of information" (imprecisely, because it is only knowledge, not ethical and aesthetic information, which is thus inflated). To aim at learning on the repertoire level does not seem, therefore, to be a very good strategy. Our memories are already filled with too many messages of knowledge. We are no longer able to manipulate that mass so well, and re-arrange it for the reception of new information. Further knowledge in such a situation is becoming useless. We cannot understand it. There are artificial memories with capacities of storage much greater than is the human one, for instance libraries, but libraries are slow and clumsy. However, recently, a revolution in memories has occurred: computers. Their storage capacity is even greater than is the library capacity: it is practically infinite (because memories can be replaced by other ones, if they are exhausted), and they are quick and handy. To store new information in computers and similar cybernetic systems, is therefore, a far better strategy than to store them in human memories. Human memory can never hope to compete with computers as far as storing is concerned. Our learning process must shift from the level of repertoire to the structural one. We must concentrate on changing the structure of our memories for the reception of various types of messages of knowledge, rather than trying to store them. We must become, all of us, "systems' analysts," rather than trying to become second-rate computers. § This implies a profound revolution in all our learning habits, including those of our school system. We cannot go on ignoring the information inflation on the one hand, and the existence of computers on the other. Admittedly, it is a painful revolution. For centuries, or even millennia, to learn meant chiefly to store information. The ideal was someone who knew everything to be known, "*uomo universale.*" Now such an ideal has become absurd. But, paradoxically, computers are now precisely such "*uomini universali."* We must abandon that ideal. Instead, we must learn structures: empty, formal disciplines, like logics, mathematics, computer languages; theories like the theory of information, decision-making, and cybernetics. In sum: we must abandon the model "what to know," and shift to the model "how to know." Our aim must not be, "to know what," but "to know how." If we go on ignoring the information inflation and the existence of computers, we shall in fact abdicate from all knowledge. We shall be manipulated by those few who have learned how to manipulate structures, and therefore use computers. We shall end up knowing nothing and being the object of somebody else's knowledge. This is the epistemological aspect of the danger of technocratic totalitarianism. § We know, of course, that this is so. The crisis of our universities is here to prove it. We know the uselessness of acquiring large amounts of knowledge. Not only because of the reasons already quoted, but also because the information inflation renders obsolete most knowledge very quickly. A student graduated in 1975 is "worth" much more than one graduated in 1945 because most of the 1945 knowledge is no longer "valid." He should therefore earn a better salary when leaving school than 10 years later. But although we know all this, we have not yet succeeded in even imagining what this new learning process is about, which is a challenge, and unless we meet it, technocrats will take over.

§ Of course: messages of knowledge are useless without messages of ethics and aesthetics. Computers are competent for knowledge only. They are mere tools. But unless we take over, unless we learn how to learn, then computers, and the technocrats who are like them, will take over. This is why we must come to understand the importance of learning how to learn to understand. *

§ For didactic purposes, messages may
be classified into those that communicate
knowledge, those that communicate desires,
and those that communicate feelings, and
such a classification is not based upon psychological criteria, but upon an analysis of
the message's structure. In this lecture I shall
concentrate upon messages of the second
class, upon what may be called the communication of ethical, or moral, values. But the
moment we consider any such message in
a concrete sense, our structural criteria fail
us. We expect desires to be communicated
in the imperative form, since "Come here!"
is an abbreviated form of "I want you to
come here." And we expect, therefore, the
class of messages we are considering to
consist of more-or-less general imperatives;
of commandments. However, we shall find
that this is not so, and that most desires are
communicated in an apparently indicative
form. To illustrate this difficulty, consider
these two messages: "Thou shalt not kill!"
and "If you kill, you risk going to jail." The

first is an abbreviation of "I want you not to kill." But the second seems to have nothing to do with a desire being communicated. It seems to be the communication of a knowledge about a situation, namely about a legal situation. Still, the second example is a communication of the same desire the first one communicates, namely: "I want you not to kill." It hides its imperative behind a façade of an implication: "if … then" to create the impression of free choice in the receiver of the message, and thus have them do what I want them to do. The reduction of these apparent implications; of these *"modes d'emploi,"* to the imperatives they are in fact, and to thus demonstrate that they belong to the class of ethical messages, is an important task of the theory of communication: "de-ideologisation." This has become increasingly important at present, because mass media are, at bottom, channels to communicate the desires of their proprietors under the mask of *"modes d'emploi"*: masked behavioural patterns. § Let me restate the problem: *this is not only a question of "grammar."* If I am able to show that the *"mode d'emploi"* printed on a tin of Maggi soup has the hidden message: "I want you to buy me," I did not merely manipulate sentence structures. This question involves the problem of values (or, the "crisis of values"). At first glance it does not seem at all as if the message, "Love thy God!" and the message, "if you open the tin, put its contents in a plate and heat it, you will have chicken soup" are of the same class. Namely: messages of behavioural patterns desired by someone. That those two messages are in fact of the same class, that they are both "ethical," namely practical models, can only be seen after a long and painful process called the "history of Western Civilisation." And it can be seen with some clarity only at present, in our situation where mass media have become the channels of communication for the desires of a technocratic and apparent "value-free" apparatus, which is the problem I want to discuss in this lecture. § At the base of our civilisation stand the Jewish and Greek traditions. For the Jewish tradition there is an eternal, transcendent Will that communicates itself to us in the form of

"revealed" behavioural models, of Commandments. These imperatives, contained
in the Bible, are very general behavioural
patterns, but it is possible to deduce very
specific models from them, models for each
and every concrete living situation. This is
done by the endless Bible commentaries, like
the Talmud. And Jewish life is "good" if it is
modelled by the elaborate deductions from
the Divine commandments in every detail.
For the Greek tradition there are eternal,
unchangeable forms, "Ideas" which stand
in Heaven. Wisdom, "*Sophia*," is to discover
those forms and to follow them in one's
living. The method for discovery is contemplation, "*Theoria*," and the application of the
forms to life is the art of mathematics and
music. The eternally supreme form is the
form of beauty and goodness, "*Kalokagathia*."
When these two traditions come together
to constitute Western Civilisation, a sort of
synthetic behavioural model comes about,
Christ, and for more than a thousand years
to live "well" is to follow that enormous and
all-embracing model: "*imitatio Christi*."
§ At the beginning of the Modern Age a

profound change occurs in Western thinking with regard to models. They are no longer taken to be a message from "outside," to be either revealed or discovered, and they are no longer taken to be unchangeable and eternal. They are now seen to be human products, instruments for the understanding of the world. This profound change occurs at first in the field of science, where models not for behaviour, but for knowledge are concerned. "Theory" thus no longer means the contemplation of eternal mathematical forms, but the elaboration of ever "better" models. But very soon this change irradiates into the field of ethics and politics as well. "The good" is no longer taken as an expression of a superhuman Will, or as an eternal "value," but as a kind of convention between humans to be constantly elaborated. At the beginning of the Modern Age, it is true, "the good" is being conceived as something to be discovered in "nature," and a sort of "natural society," "natural law," and "natural behaviour" are searched for. But soon this transposition of ethical models from the transcendent into the immanent is abandoned in favour of a radical reformulation of the concept of "model." Essentially, this is what the word "modern" means: the progressive elaboration of ever "better" models of behaviour, knowledge, and experience; of ever "better" *modes d'emploi*; of ever improving "modes" = fashions. The belief in progress, which characterises the Modem Age, the belief that it is possible to understand the world ever better, and to change it ever better, and to build ever better societies according to ever better social models, and so forth, is fundamentally the belief that models are human instruments capable of constant improvement. We are now at the end of the Modern Age, because we no longer hold that belief: we do not know what is meant by the term "a better model." § It has become clear to us that the Modern concept of "model" is in fact a hybrid: on the one hand Modern thinkers accept it to be a fact that models are human products, but on the other hand they still hold that they are some kind of approximation of some "definitive," "perfect" model. Which is what is meant by "improvement":

an approximation of the perfect model. This is true for scientific models: they are "better" if they approach "truer knowledge." And this is true for ethical models: they are "better" if they approach "perfect society" and the "good life." Thus, to be "Modern" is to have pushed the eternal model from the centre to the horizon: a model that cannot be followed, but which may be approached by infinite progression. The Moderns did not abolish the concept of an "eternal, perfect model" they only made it inoperative. But we, for many reasons that cannot be discussed here, have been obliged to abandon such a concept completely. The term "a better model" is for us a meaningless term. For us, every model is "good" for the purpose it was intended: nothing is "good in itself," and everything is "good for something." Brigitte Bardot is a good model for soap-buying behaviour, and soap buying is a good model for consumer behaviour, and consumer behaviour is a good model for life in an industrial society, and so forth. On the other hand terrorism is a good model for revolutionary behaviour, and revolutionary

behaviour is a good model for social change,
and social change is a good model for new
types of production, and so forth. There is,
for us, no sense in saying that Miss Bardot is
a better or worse model than Mr. Che Gue-
vara, unless we say that it is better for something somebody wants somewhere. And that
is what is commonly called "the crisis of
values." § What I have just said is of course
an exaggeration. None of us is in fact completely "beyond Good and Evil," yet. But if
I say, "generals are as good for killing as
Maggi soups are good for eating" you will
probably smile, which is a sign that you still
believe in some sort of hierarchy of values.
Some pale ghost of the Divine Will and of
Kalokagathia still lingers on in the background
of our conscience. The reason is, of course,
that we are not yet beyond values, but within
the crisis of values. We are no longer strictly
Moderns, but still: not everything is for us a
mere question of fashion. And those of us
who are almost beyond values, namely the
technocrats and their functionaries (those of
us who indeed no longer believe in "objective values"), are themselves in trouble to

cling to their newly conquered pragmatism.
They may proclaim themselves to be "value-free," but still, they know that they are at
the service of some Will which is "ideologi-
cal" in the sense of believing to be, itself, in
some way "objective." This dichotomy of
ours, this being and not-being "Moderns,"
this tendency towards "de-ideologisation,"
but also towards commitment, in short: this
confusion of ours as far as behavioural
models are concerned, is reflected in our
daily scene, but of course most obviously, in
our communication. § From this point of
view an analysis of the messages within mass
media becomes revealing. On the one hand
we shall find messages that proclaim, very
elegantly, some traditional "behavioural"
models, like love for each other and for God,
patriotism and progress towards socialism,
kindness towards widows and children, and
so forth. It does not matter very much that
some of those models are in conflict with
others: this "defence of Western values" is
only a surface phenomenon, and the imperatives thus communicated are only a pretext
for more meaningful communication.

Namely, the communication of *"modes d'emploi"* that are behavioural models in the interest of those who own mass media channels. These *"modes d'emploi"* are masked under the form of implications such as "if ... then," but also under the form of epistemological and aesthetic models. Miss Bardot appears in the media apparently as an actress, therefore, as an aesthetic model. But she is, of course, in reality, an ethical model, a model for consumer behaviour, and this is the reason why she is shown on TV and in films. The communication of *"modes d'emploi"* is the real purpose of mass communication, and the *"modes d'emploi"* are the true values to which those media are committed. This becomes clear under analysis; under "de-ideologisation." The dichotomy is in the fact that fashion, *"mode d'emploi,"* becomes, somehow, an ideology in its own right. In fact, and paradoxically, it becomes the ideology of the apparently ideology-free technocratic apparatus. Although all imperatives seem to have been "overcome," they may be re-discovered behind apparently value-free implications. § The choice we are being offered at present is not, as it appears to be, one between traditional values, no longer believed in, and a value-free life, within which we may elaborate our own specific and pragmatic models. Rather, we are being presented a choice between traditional values and values that are not ours but of those who hold power of decision, although we try to hide this. And there is, in fact, no true choice. Seldom, if ever, has there been so little freedom of choice as at present. We slip into behavioural patterns, into the fashions proposed to us, without being aware of it. And if we look at our scene, where fashions seem to change very quickly, but where fundamental patterns tend to become ever more rigid, we may appreciate this danger. Every year a new model of Renault is proposed to us, and every year we become more conditioned by the motorcar model. No doubt: we cannot go back to the Bible in the sense of accepting "perfect models." But no doubt also: we cannot accept Miss Bardot and the fashions that precede and follow her as a solution of our crisis of values. I have no idea how to solve such crisis. If I had, there would be no crisis. But what I can do is to put the problem before you within the terms of the theory of communication: the problem is in the translation of apparent *implications* into the *imperatives* they are at heart. You will have seen, if you have followed this lecture, that this is not a question of grammar, but of existential suffering. *

Vilém Flusser

§ One of the basic limitations of communicability is the fact that concrete experience cannot be communicated. This is so, because to communicate is to generalise, both in the sense of *to compare,* and *to make public;* and also, because "concrete experience" means precisely that which can be compared with none other, and which cannot be made public. Concrete experience is, by definition, unique and private. Still: there can be no doubt that our concrete experiences of the world are, to a large extent, informed by what is vaguely called "our cultural condition." Take the concrete experience of love between a man and a woman as an example. This can never be generalised: each such experience is unique and private, and cannot therefore be communicated. Still: we feel, while experiencing it, that we are being conditioned, and that this conditioning comes from two levels. One level may be called the "natural" one (the one of our physical, chemical, physiological, and so forth, conditions) and we need not go into that during this lecture.

But the other level of conditioning, the "cultural" one, is far more interesting. It may be shown that we love the woman we love within very specific historical patterns, which lie in our memories, in our "program." It may be shown that the pattern "love between the sexes" is not universal for mankind (there are societies that do not have it, and where the concrete experience of this love is therefore impossible), and that it is a pattern that changes during the history of our own culture. In Classical times, for instance, love between the sexes was considered to be a vulgar pragmatic affair, because it resulted in children and was therefore not a "pure" experience. The only "true" love was the homosexual one, which we now call "Platonic." During the Middle Ages, two types of love between the sexes were being distinguished: "high" love between a Lady and a Knight (the model of which was the love of St. Mary), and "low" love between a girl (or more frequently a married woman) and a poet. The relationship between husband and wife did not fit well into any of those two patterns. During the late Middle

Ages, under the influence of the *Roman de la Rose*, our present model of love between man and woman began to be elaborated, and it is called "Romantic" because of that work of art. This model took a very long time to penetrate into the concrete experience of the "masses." Even as late as Romanticism, this was still an experience restricted only to the bourgeoisie. Today, this is a common experience, thanks to cheap novels, films, and television. Although each of us is having a unique, private, and incommunicable experience of love for a man or a woman, still, we have this experience within models that have been communicated to us over time. § I have elaborated this example somewhat excessively, because it can show what "art" is: the composition and communication of models for our concrete experiences of the world. It may be shown that we experience everything within such models, and that we are programmed for all our pleasures and pains; for all colours, sounds, shapes, and textures; for all perfumes, and for all our loves and hates through art. This is one of the basic differences between animals and Man: our concrete world is structured not only by our genetic program, but also by what may be called, our "aesthetic" program (if by "aesthetic" we mean what the word etymologically implies, namely *"aistheton"* = concrete experience). Where there is no aesthetic model available, we are literally "anaesthetised" = we experience nothing. We depend on art to experience the world. Art is our method to perceive what is "real." Art is responsible for the fact that our world is a *"Lebenswelt"* (a world of human life) and not, like it is for animals, an *"Umwelt"* (an ecological system). In other words: art programs us for the experience of reality, and artists are our reality programmers, just as in the case of computers, where there are those who program them for specific calculations. The case in point is not only that we see a landscape within the model of a Leonardo or a Turner: rather, where there is no landscape painter there is no landscape. Human reality is a product of art (love and landscape just as much as war and the molecule of ribonucleic acid), and art is *"poiesis"*: the pro-duction of what is real. § There seems

to be a curious contradiction here: on the
one hand it is impossible to communicate
the concrete experiences we are having. And
on the other, there seems to be no concrete
experience without a model that has been
communicated. However, the fact is simple:
models of concrete experience ("works of
art" in common language) are not generali-
sations of the artist's experience, and cannot
be it. They are structures, forms, patterns
(or whatever the term we may choose) that
the artist proposes for our future concrete
experiences of the world. A love poem is not
a generalisation of a specific experience of
love the poet had: it is a proposal of how to
experience love within a form not yet uti-
lised in the past. A musical composition or
an impressionist painting is not a generalisation of a concrete experience of sound or
colour the artist had, but a proposal of how
to experience sound and colour (and the
feelings, ideas, and wishes connected with
such an experience) within a new pattern.
Artists do not try to communicate their
private experiences; make a sort of confes-
sion. This would be an impossible, and also

a very dull, undertaking. They submit pro-
posals for future experience patterns. Their
aim is to make reality richer. And in fact
they are not so much concerned with what
they are themselves experiencing, as with
previous experience models. A poem of love
has not so much to do with the love the poet
is feeling as with the poem of love he was
reading. § If what I said is true, if artists are
indeed, in the saying of Heidegger's, "the
organs by which we devour reality," it is
obvious that aesthetic communication must
precede ethical and epistemological communication. We can only judge what we have
experienced, and we can only know what we
have experienced and judged. The artist is
the producer of the stuff (namely "reality")
that the politician judges and the scientist
investigates. But of course the division into
art, politics, and science is the product of a
schizophrenic mentality, called "Modern
Civilisation." In fact, there is no such division. Every human communication is aesthetic, ethical, and epistemological at the
same time. Every scientist is also an artist
and a politician, every politician is also a

scientist and an artist, and every artist is also a scientist and a politician. The endless talk about politically committed or uncommitted art, or about a type of art that is dependent or independent of science and its techniques, is nonsense. As much nonsense as is the endless talk about the "value freedom" of science. And it shows why Jews, Christians, and Muslims have that curious idea that beauty may be sinful (I shall come back to this later). In short: every human communication is an aesthetic one, as it always transmits a model for concrete experience, and in this sense, we are all artists. In the words of a poet: *Man walks wrapped in beauty, and wherever he steps, he creates beauty.*

§ And this permits us to say what is the meaning of the word "beauty": it means the originality, the newness, of an aesthetic proposition. A model of concrete experience is "beautiful" to the extent to which there is no other previous model just like it, therefore, to the extent to which this model makes reality richer. "Beauty" is thus synonymous with "increasing the parameters of experience of the real," which seems to be a very empirical definition of beauty. And it is this empiricism of the definition that has rendered art criticism so dubious: "*de gustibus non est disputandum.*" But we now have a theory (the theory of information) that permits us to define beauty far better. We may now say that the beauty of an aesthetic proposition (of a "work of art") is equal to the amount of information it contains (which could, as a thesis, but not always in praxis, be calculated). Therefore, art criticism may, at long last, become more than the mere exclamation "I like this!" And the theory of information has the advantage of being able to show us the central problem of artistic communication: that if it contains too little information, if it is too "traditional," it is not beautiful (reality is not enriched by it). But if artistic communication contains too much information, if it does not absorb a sufficient amount of redundancy from traditional models, it does not communicate and becomes useless (again, reality is not enriched by it). The artist's problem is to walk the narrow path between banality (Kitsch) and redundancy (excess of information). The famous dichotomy: folly/ genius. § But if beauty is originality, we may understand why our established religions (and other ideologies) mistrust beauty and the artist. Religions are the keepers of established behavioural models (of ethical values). If our models of experience change through the propositions of beauty, then behavioural models are bound to change with them. Art is the true medium of revolution (in politics as much as it is in science). If our experience of reality changes, everything else changes. This is the reason why "pure beauty" is sinful, and why the Soviets put artists into asylums. In other words: for established ideologies it is not nice to propose beauty. And since we are, all of us, ideologically programmed, we agree with them. Indeed: beauty is not nice. It is highly disagreeable, to say the least. And, to say it better: beauty is terrifying. Rilke says that beauty is the beginning of terror, which we can stand only because beauty does not want to destroy us. But beauty *is* terrifying, precisely because it proposes to change our experience of the real. It shouts at us: "*Du must dein Leben ändern!* = You must change your life!" It is far more agreeable to try and ignore beauty, and concentrate upon the nice old models, which are nice because they are old and we are already programmed by them. Mozart is much nicer than Schönberg, and Dante much nicer than Cummings, because the reality that Mozart and Dante propose is one for which we are pro-grammed. Of course: Mozart and Dante were definitely not nice in their times. They have become nice through time; they have become redundant. But even so: they may be dangerous. Because they have proposed so much information, that time may not even now have exhausted it. At present, it is far better if we trust those who propose models that repeat Mozart and Dante. They are much nicer. We can calmly enjoy them. They confirm our patterns of experience, instead of proposing new ones. Kitsch is the nicest. And it has a further advantage: Kitsch may serve as a mask for behavioural patterns. If our patterns of experience are maintained steady, we can be more easily manipulated, which is the reason and the Justification for mass art. § Mass media are thus committed to Kitsch by their very function, which establishes, at present, a curious vicious circle. On the one hand mass media are nice: they confirm our established patterns of experience. We love like Hollywood, we see colours like Kodak, and we weep like the Blues. On the other hand mass media force all those who want to propose new experience models into closed, highly hermetic circuits. Thus "avant-garde" art, amputated from society by mass media, becomes far too "beautiful" (too rich in information) and can communicate nothing. This pernicious division of art into nice mass art and beautiful elitist art is a new phenomenon, and may result in a not as yet imaginable "death of the arts," namely, stagnation of experience, which means total alienation. This will be the subject of a future lecture. Let me end by saying that beauty is what characterises human communication: beauty is a structuring, namely the endowing of significance, to human existence. If art is, as they say, in crisis, human existence *"tout court"* is in crisis. The first witness of Man on Earth is beauty, namely: information. If art should die, then entropy, nature, would take over. Because this is what art is: the contrary of nature. And this is what Man is: a being contrary to nature, an artificial-being, and an artist. We walk in beauty. *

THE AVANT-GARDE AND
CLOSED CIRCUIT COMMUNICATION

§ The communication revolution that is
the theme of this course of lectures has
profoundly changed the structure of what
may be called "our cultural system." We
may consider the culture we live in to be a
system composed of elements (culturemes)
that are ordered by rules (structure). During
the last three lectures I tried to suggest how
the communication revolution has affected
our culturemes (our models of knowledge,
behavior, and experience) and it is to the
change of structure caused by such revolution that I want to draw your attention
today. Roughly speaking, the structure
of the Western cultural system before the
revolution was organised into three levels:
popular, national, and universal culture.
Each level had its specific character, and
they were in specific communication with
each other. Popular culture was a memory
within which models elaborated on the
other levels were stored in a more-or-less
prehistorical, mythical structure. Universal
culture (which meant: common to the West)

was the historical discourse composed of
dialogues that elaborated models. And
national culture was a more or less deliberate
and artificial middle layer of rather recent
origin (a product of the bourgeois school
system, therefore of the invention of printing), which complicated the function of the
cultural system without contributing anything to it. That system worked more or less
as follows: on the universal level there were
those who had learned the codes that char-
acterise Western culture. Those codes were
responsible for the progressive, historical
dynamism of that level. New models were
being constantly evolved in science, politics,
and the arts, and this elaboration was a
more-or-less deliberate process. We may
distinguish the following phases: Renais-
sance, Mannerism, Baroque, Enlightenment,
Romanticism, Realism, and ever-shorter
phases, more difficult to be distinguished
due to the acceleration of progress. In the
case of politics (and to some extent, in the
case of art) but not in the case of science,
models were translated into the somewhat
simpler and cruder codes of the national

level of culture: there were national politics, to some extent national arts, but never a national science. On that level not much more was done than the transmission of those cruder models to a greater number of receivers (to the participants of schools and similar institutions), through discourse. And the models elaborated on the universal level were also translated into the entirely different codes of the popular level, both directly and through the intermediary of the national level. Two things happened during that translation: the models were changed, sometimes very profoundly, and there was a time gap (*déphasage*) between the elaboration of the model and its reception on the popular level. Thus a scientific model may have become a myth when reaching the popular level, and popular culture may have been Baroque whilst the universal level was changing into Romanticism. There was, however, a constant feedback between the various levels. Since all participants of the universal level also participated in the popular one, they were constantly being informed by it. And when the Industrial Revolution challenged that feedback by creating the big proletarian towns, the Western cultural system tried to save itself by absorbing the proletarians into the national level, and by artificially (Romantically) trying to keep the popular level alive. This succeeded, more-or-less, until the Second World War, although the West paid a terrible price for it.

§ The Western cultural system is the result of the revolution caused by the invention of printing, which disrupted Catholicism's cultural system, with relatively little feedback from other contemporary systems, although of course some Eastern and African elements did penetrate the West. But the West's discursive dynamism, especially as far as scientific models are concerned, was responsible, in its later stages, for what is called "Western Imperialism." During the nineteenth century, the Western cultural system dominated the Earth and disrupted all other cultural systems, without being itself very much informed by them. The Western universal level became thus truly "universal," although in a tyrannical sense of the term, and at the same time the popular level of Western Civilisation became slowly disrupted, almost just as much as non-Western cultures, and degraded into folklore. Around the middle of the twentieth century, the Western system's terminal stage was structured approximately like this: it had a highly dynamic, ever more rapidly progressive universal level, an increasingly vulgarised, impoverished, proletarian national level, and a rapidly decaying and artificially maintained popular level. At this point, the mass media revolution set in, destroying the very foundations of the West's cultural system by degrading the alphabetic printed code to become only one among many codes of prevailing communication. In a very short time it swept away the national level of culture by substituting the level of mass culture for it (which will be the subject of the next lecture). But by doing so, and for other reasons, it also profoundly changed the structure of the universal level of culture. This is the situation we find ourselves in at present: there is a truly universal, namely global, level of culture, whereon our models are being elaborated, but it has an entirely different structure from what it had before the communication revolution. There is an equally universal level of mass culture, whereon the models of the universal level are being impressed, and there are mass media that transmit the models from the upper to the lower level without any true feedback. Therefore, our cultural system has become far simpler, and it works incomparably better. Thus, it has become more impoverished. § What characterises the upper level is the high degree of elaboration of its various codes, and the difficulty of translating from one into another. However, these levels are not being disrupted only into two cultures (as C.P. Snow thought), into the scientific and humanistic ones, with very little communication between them. The disruption goes much deeper. The code of nuclear physics is so different from the code of economics (let alone from the code of poetry or filmmaking) that any effort to translate from one to the other seems misguided. One may thus speak of an explosive fission of our culture on the upper level, which consists of small clots of culturemes that fly in various directions away from each other and break up again in the process. This is true for scientific models, of course, but almost as true for aesthetic models. Such an explosion no longer merits the term "progress": it has made a qualitative jump from previous development, and has become different. Simultaneously it has become increasingly difficult to learn any one of the codes with which upper communication functions, and this learning process may take up much of the lifetime of those who participate in it. This again is the reason why the upper level of our culture has become hermetically closed to the vast majority. Higher education has never before been so widely distributed as it is now, which seems to suggest that many more now participate in higher culture than before the communication revolution. But this is an illusion. In reality, all those millions of university students, art students, and so forth, are mere candidates for participation in any type of meaningful dialogue, and shall never "make it." § The upper level of culture is at present divided up into a great number of small committees, of closed circuits, which elaborate ever more refined models without any true communication with even the next committee right beside it. The models thus elaborated are directly available only to those very few who have learned its code, and who stand, more-or-less passively, around the committee in session. (We can have a good image of that situation if we look at an art exhibition. But the same is of course true for scientific laboratories, technical symposia, and international economic meetings). It is easy to say that this is a characteristically "elitist" situation, like it existed for instance in hierarchic Egypt. But our situation is different. Not only is the elite at present alienated from what now may be called for the first time correctly "the masses," but each elitist group is also alienated from all other elite groups. And every further progress in such a situation means further alienation. In other terms: the various dialogues that go on at this level of culture result in an enormous amount of information that is more-or-less useless, because there is no

appropriate code to transmit it to other
dialogic groups (let alone to the masses).
This information inflation was already
mentioned in a previous lecture. § Paradoxically, however, the chaotic state of high
culture, an entropy due to excessive information, is being sucked in and transformed
into an amorphous steady flow by that meat
grinder called "mass media." All those
mutually incommunicable models are being
translated into very simple *"modes d'emploi"* by
being recodified into the codes of TV,
magazines, commercial advertising, and so
forth. To understand this miracle, two things
must be considered: One has to do with the
fact that the upper level of our culture has
become highly "value free"; it elaborates
very few behavioural models for reasons
discussed here under the heading "the crisis
of values." Mass media are therefore free to
transform all epistemological and aesthetic
models into ethical models. The other thing
has to do with the highly connotative quality of the codes of mass communication.
Such codes are capable of translating almost
all messages into an amorphous broth, into

that "night in which all the cows are gray."
Thus, mass media guarantee the simple
unity of our culture by translating all the
highly refined models of the upper level into
very simple, universally valid *"modes d'emploi"*
that structure our mass culture. And they
can do so, because the manipulation of mass
media has itself become the result of one of
those hermetic dialogues that go on at the
upper level. Dissemination (vulgarisation)
has become, itself, a highly refined and
exactly codified discipline performed within
a closed circuit. The open broadcasting
systems of mass culture are programmed
within closed circuits. § Currently, this
seems to be an extremely stable cultural
system: a perfect domination of the lower by
the upper level. Fortunately this is not so,
because the system lacks feedback. This
system is an uninterrupted discourse from
the higher towards the lower level, and all its
dialogues are restricted to closed circuits on
the upper level. This lack of feedback, this
alienation, of each part of the system from
any other, is the system's weakness, since it
renders the system vulnerable to internal and

external disturbances. Cybernetics shows why this is so, and if we reflect upon those formal reasons for our culture's vulnerability, then such weakness may be experienced in our own lives. We are frustrated by our culture, whether we participate in mass culture, or whether we attempt to participate (rather, have the opportunity to attempt to participate) in elite culture. The frustration of the masses will be the subject of our next lecture. The frustration of the elite is due to its growing feeling of isolation. Only very few intimates receive the models one elaborates, and if they are disseminated, we no longer recognise them as ours. We cannot "realise" ourselves in such a situation, unless we become specialists, which means no longer fully human. Of course, our situation may come to transform us into something no longer human. But as long as it does not succeed in this, our frustration may be explosive. We may yet succeed in changing our culture before it changes us. And some of the methods by which that may be done have been discussed in this course of lectures. I shall go back to them in the next lecture. Let me end here by saying that the avant-garde, in the sense of participation in closed circuit communication, is in fact the rear-guard of our cultural system. *

ALIENATION AND STEREOTYPE

§ Last week I proposed a way of looking at our cultural system, and analysed its "upper" level. Today, I propose a way of looking at our "mass culture." This term, "mass," which in the past meant the majority of the population, only now acquires its etymological meaning. Which means that, for the first time in history, a colossal number of people (more than three billion) cover the Earth like a continuously growing moss. This mass is amorphous, in the sense that it has lost the structures that informed it up until only a few decades ago: different popular cultures. Therefore, the mass has become the raw material upon which mass media impress the behavioural models elaborated by elite culture. Consequently, the mass is quite literally, "a dough." Due to its qualitative aspect (the amorphous and mobile plasticity of this human moss, and the globally irradiating structure of mass media) the mass has become a new historical fact. If nothing intervenes, in the near future the Earth will be covered by a mass made up of dozens of billions of people who will behave, globally, according to a few specific universal stereotypes. Initially, I shall consider the quantitative aspect of this.

§ The so-called demographic explosion is not only the increase of the number of people on Earth, which means, therefore, a violent change in how humanity relates to this Earth (ecology), and of human relations (economy and sociology). It also means a radical change in the concept of what it is to be Human (anthropology), because the concept that we have of what it is to be Human is not only due to our experiences as individual humans, but also due to our global view of humanity. Certainly, the type of anthropology that deals with billions of people must necessarily be different to the type of anthropology that deals with tens of billions of people (as is the case of traditional anthropology), which means a significant qualitative leap, thus, the concept of "Man" changes. And this change needs to be accepted, as hard as it may be, since this is not the first time in history that such a leap has come about: the transition from the Palaeolithic to the Mesolithic is an example. At that point, hunters were counted in the hundreds and farmers in the thousands, which must have revolutionised anthropology. And, of course, there were also other, comparable anthropological crises in the course of history. One cannot overestimate the effects of quantitative leaps upon our concepts. When history is measured in millions of years instead of thousands, the concept of history changes. When space is measured in light-years instead of thousands of kilometres, the concept of space changes. Thus, it becomes inevitable that the term "Human" acquires a revolutionary new meaning at present, which is, therefore, one of the challenges that the crisis in which we find ourselves posits.

§ One cannot deny, as difficult as it may be, that value is a result of frequency. The more numerous a species is, the lesser is the value of one of its individuals, not only in an economic sense: it is cheaper to substitute one individual by another (it is cheaper to substitute a pebble than a diamond). But also in an existential sense: an individual of

a rare species is more interesting than an
individual of a common species (to find a
cow is less interesting than to find a giraffe).
The demographic explosion turns humans
more frequent, more "common," and dimin-
ishes their value, their dignity. Not only
"objectively" but also "subjectively": it
becomes increasingly easier to substitute one
human by another, and it becomes increasingly less "strange" to meet a stranger. For a
Palaeolithic hunter, to meet a member of an
unknown horde must have been terrifying; it
would have been the experience of the
sacredness of the stranger. We can no longer
imagine a type of anthropology founded
upon such an experience of Man. The indif-
ference with which we cross once "exotic"
persons on the streets is, for our parents,
already existential proof of how much our
anthropology is changing. § The degrada-
tion of individual humans by the demographic explosion, strengthened by the great
mobility of the masses (worker, foreigner,
tourist, refugee, planned city etc.) turns our
anthropology increasingly scientific. Since
humanity has become a frequent species, we

can calculate its movements through ever more exact statistics, make predictions with lower margins of error, and manipulate these numbers with greater perfection. We can thus explain "the Human phenomenon" increasingly better, and manipulate it ever more scientifically. Therefore, this new anthropology allows for a human technique, according to the recent concept of "Human": an object of research and manipulation. Thanks to its quantitative growth, the mass is becoming a type of scientifically explainable and manipulable raw material. And this is a new thing. § We have difficulty in admitting this, because traditional anthropology (the so-called "Humanist" one) is still active in our memories. We refuse to see the reality of the masses. We continuously want to apply our old categories (nation, class, race etc.) so as to deny the amorphous reality of the masses, even if these categories work progressively worse. Or, we propose new categories, so as to create distinctions in the mass, and thus, somehow save the individual's dignity. For example: by opposing "third world" and "developed countries" as categories. This is already a type of capitulation before such reality. We are ready to admit that high culture is universal: it makes no sense in trying to deny that a Hindu or Nigerian biologist belongs to the same culture as an American or Russian biologist. But we insist on there being a difference between the culture of a Hindu or Nigerian peasant and that of an American or Russian worker. However, this reality negates even such a desperate effort to find a structure in the amorphous mass. Nevertheless, it is a fact that the economic and social reality of the Hindu or Nigerian peasant is completely different to the economic and social reality of the American or Russian worker, and effectively, the abyss between these realities always increases. However, the culture in which these four people find themselves, the culture of the mass, is exactly the same wherever they are. All four of them see the world through Kodak colours, love like in Hollywood films, drink Coca-Cola, and also dream of the conquest of Mars. Mass culture does not allow for the application of categories; it becomes progressively more

amorphous. § Here's a fundamental fact:
The economic, social, and political
differences between the impoverished
majority and the never before imagined
opulent lifestyle of the minority continues
to grow, and even so, they all participate in
the same mass culture. In other words:
culture almost no longer has any relation to
the economic, social, and political reality.
This is an alienated culture that also
alienates us from such realities: the conquest
of Mars, as a model, can hardly be adapted
to the reality of an American or Russian
worker, or to that of a Hindu and Nigerian
peasant. The degree of alienation of all four
of them is the same. The models impressed
upon the masses by communication media
are independent from the reality of the
mass. That is why the mass can no longer
"find itself" within its reality. § This divorce
between model and reality (between the
conquest of Mars and the rice harvest), is
due to the lack of feedback between elaboration and model (the prototype), and the
application of the model upon the mass (the
stereotype), which is a reformulation of

what I spoke in the last lecture about the lack of feedback between elite and mass cultures. Such feedback did exist in the Western cultural system, but it was destroyed by the communication revolution. High culture was "historical" and popular culture was "prehistorical," however, feedback always obliged history to return to its popular roots. Extra-Western cultural systems, destroyed by the West, undoubtedly also had feedback between their different cultural levels. And whichever were the dialectic tensions that characterised the Western system, endowing it with a specific dynamic, were probably not so strong. However, the current cultural system no longer has feedback, therefore, it no longer has dialectic contradiction. There is no longer any feedback between prototype and stereotype. § Consequently, the way that the mass behaves becomes a reflex, conditioned by the models elaborated at the upper level of culture. The hotdog, guerrilla, shampoo, or kidnapping models are not affected by their application. Whether we eat a hotdog in Aix-en-Provence or Calcutta; make guerrilla in Angola or Berlin; buy shampoo at a supermarket in São Paulo or Reykjavík, or take hostages in Rome or Djibouti, the models are the same: stereotypes of prototypes. And still, we obviously, cannot admit this. The technicians at McDonald's seem to run focus groups to adapt the hotdog to the consumers' wishes. The guerrilla planners seem to want to adapt their model to the reality in Angola or Berlin. But that is an illusion; they cannot do it, since the mass does not have means at its disposal in order to communicate anything in face of the univocal structure of mass media. The mass limits itself to applying prototypes in a stereotypical way, through conditioned reflexes. And that is why models are at work everywhere. § The elaboration of prototypical models is always "historical," in the sense that it is progressive and processual, despite the lack of feedback, since elite culture finds itself at the centrifugal explosion of which I spoke last time. However, the stereotypical application of models has become "post-historical," in the sense that it is only a historical reflex, and as for the mass, it becomes a passive object of such history. But the mass moves, of course, and it moves more violently and widely than ever before, however, it moves towards stereotypes. That is why such movements are not historical movements, "actions," but reflected movements, "reactions." Consequently, the most violent movements such as wars, plunders, mutinies etc. continue to be possible, and even more frequent than ever before. However, historical movements, such as revolutions, are no longer possible. That is why we are entering post-history. § Evidently, it is possible that this divorce between mass culture and the reality in which the mass lives, this monumental alienation, ends in an unimaginable explosion. But that is very unlikely, since the illusion created by mass media through the new audiovisual codes and their discursive irradiation is so perfect that this illusion becomes more real than reality. The illusion of having a haircut like that of Miss Bardot is more real than the reality of the family, and the illusion of Angola's independence is more real than the reality of its economic catastrophe. The mass has no conscience of its reality, and this situation is, in the final analysis, what mass media intend. If we wish to avoid stereotypes becoming eternal (as we should, in my own opinion), we need to act at the level where prototypes are elaborated. And in this sense, I repeat, our only hope lies in artistic activity. Thanks to models of concrete experience, the elite may regain contact with the reality from which it is as alienated as the masses (due to the same lack of feedback). And we will only be able to break the nefarious chain of "alienated prototype/ alienating stereotype" (which threatens to drag us into post-history) by elaborating prototypes that are open towards reality. *

CONCLUSIONS

§ This series of lectures on the phenomena of communication, which ends today, followed a very high, linear flight-path (in other words: it was superficial), high above the living, pulsating, and undulating mesh that human communication is. This has been more of a reconnaissance flight for a future strategy, and not an analysis of the mesh. We were able to notice, vaguely, the outlines of a continent bathed by entropy; the majestic peaks of scientific, ethic, and aesthetic discourses; the soft plains of amorous and philosophic dialogues, as well as the frightening abysses of demagogy and nonsense upon this living, pulsating, undulating continent that floats on the waves of absurdity and death thanks to its symbolising capacity. A continent that is an illusion, a Fata Morgana, an Atlantis, upon which we live, and which is our only homeland. Human communication is this: the illusion of the denial of nature, whose idiotic tendency tends towards the total equilibrium of entropy and death. There-

fore, human communication is the illusion
of immortality, that is, of a memory formed
by increasing symbolic information. Of
course, we know that this is an illusion, and
we know it thanks to our body's suffering:
despite our individual and collective memories, we remain mortals. Nevertheless, this
illusion is, still, our own reality, our onto-
logical dignity. And it is due to the illusion
of symbolic communication that we are
really Human. Summing up: the continent
surveyed during these lectures is the domain
upon which our lives gain significance;
become meaningful. And that is why I held
the following hypothesis during our course
of lectures: the structure of communication
is the infrastructure of human reality.
§ This hypothesis is not in any way an
idealist article of faith, or a Hegelian thesis.
In fact, I would not deny, even for one
second, that we may "explain," equally well,
our reality by using the hypothesis of an
economic, social, or psychological infrastructure (or any other type of infrastructure) as a starting point. Hence, I believe
that a hypothesis is never "true" or "false,"

because, in order to believe the opposite, it would be necessary to hold certain criteria of truth, which I do not hold. On the contrary, I believe that a hypothesis is "good" or "bad" according to the extent that it allows to be worked with. A hypothesis is a tool, not a revelation. And what I attempted to do during the course of these lectures was to show you how our situation presents itself if we assume, hypothetically, that the structure of communication is the infrastructure of human reality. § What initially draws our attention, if we assume such point of view, is the fact that the structure of human communication is, today, changing violently. If we define human communication as the process through which information travels between memories via channels, we are obliged to note that, today, there has been a revolutionary change upon memories and channels. Regarding memories, this revolution is cybernetic: computers, microfiche libraries, film and video libraries etc. And thanks to this revolution, our memories have not only become very fast and large, but have also become very difficult to manage, having the tendency to become autonomous in relation to the traditional memories that programmed them: cybernetic memories can re-program themselves, and communicate with each other without immediate interference from other traditionally "human" memories. Therefore, their codes are not the traditional ones. Regarding channels, this revolution is mass media: cinema, TV, billboards, illustrated magazines, omnipresent photographic images etc. And thanks to this revolution, our communication has become synchronic and uniform throughout the globe, since it is dominated by the structure of irradiated discourses, and so the "conceptual" codes of spoken languages find themselves on the way of being supplanted by the codes of sonorous moving images. If we assume the hypothesis according to which the structure of communication is the structure of human reality, then we are obliged to find that the reality, "Man," is changing.

§ You may object, of course, and say that such a statement is banal, since: is Man not, almost by definition, a being that changes all the time, a "historical" being? Is Man not a being that self-mutates all the time? Is Man not the symptom of a reactionary mentality that insists upon the "eternally human"? And so, is this not precisely the "pedagogical" function of communication: to teach that the son/daughter is not like the father/mother? However, if you do object, you will miss the impact of the changes in question today, because, it is not the case of a change in Man within the structure of communication, but of a change in Man *because* of a change in the structure of communication. This does not mean that a generation is different from the preceding one, but that they cannot fully communicate with each other. Currently, it is no longer the case of a historical process, but of a rupture in the historical process. § Let me restate: historically, this is not the first rupture of such nature. The invention of linear writing, which resulted in so-called *history*, was definitely a rupture comparable to ours. And certainly, there were others, even if they have been obscured by the dark night of the past and oblivion (I am referring to the "invention" of painting, music, and spoken language). However, this is a rare event, and I do not believe that the invention of the printing press, even though it was very important for the structure of communication, is of the same order as the current rupture. Certainly: such rare and deep ruptures are not mysterious events that fall upon us from up on high, miracles, or accidents. Humans, with the implicit, or even explicit, objective to change the structure of communication, were the inventors of linear writing. Humans are also the, more-or-less, conscious authors of the current rupture, of which we are witnesses and victims. However, this rupture also overcomes us. Our own inventions can dominate us, and transform us in ways we cannot predict or desire. Our instruments' tendency to become autonomous from our own Will, and to transform us into instruments of our own instruments, is Man's alienation in relation to his own creation, and is a real and well-known danger. We should not allow this to happen, but it is happening. Thus, the challenge of our rupture is that it will "change" the reality "Man" in a way we did not desire. § Perhaps it is convenient at this point to revisit the only example of a rupture comparable to ours, which is still, in some way, in our memories: linear writing. Humanity changed with linear writing. Human thought became linear, historical, processual, and conceptual, just like the alphabet. Humans invented the alphabet, and then became like their invention. And it goes further: humans and their world became "books," and linear reading became the method through which Man came to know himself and others, with whom he is in the world, as well as the world in which he finds himself. Thanks to linear writing, Man finds himself as a book amongst books, and linear mathematics, logics, and historical action; messianic thinking, utopias, the concept of progress, and the ethic of "the new," are only some examples of the change that the invention of linear writing caused in Man. I also believe that our brains have changed, and that there are now "writing" nodes within them. The Sumerian inventors of linear writing could have predicted none of these changes. So

Man changes himself, but is this any consolation? § Let us consider this: we are illiterates in relation to future Man, in the same way that the Sumerian scribes were illiterates in relation to us. They knew how to write, of course, just as we know how to program TVs and computers. However, realistically speaking, they did not write, they translated traditional, prehistoric messages such as bas-relief, sculpture, dance, and oral narrative codes into the alphabetic code. They did not dominate the alphabet, and did not know what to do with it. We do not know what to do with our new memories and mass media communication. And this ignorance about the instruments we have invented is where the danger lies. These instruments will change us against our will unless we dominate them. As humanity became like the alphabet, humans dominated it. This was a long and arduous process, which has not been fully consummated. Or, maybe we fool ourselves: is it possible that humanity has never dominated the alphabet; that humanity has become just like the alphabet for not having dominated it, and that we are not aware of this because we have been dominated, possessed, by the alphabet? However, in any case, there was a period in Egypt during which undominated writing threatened humanity with deathly mummification. The Temple Scribes (whose monumental expressions, fixed upon statues, we can still admire) petrified their society for quite some years. And Pharaonic tyranny, or in other words, an un-alphabetically prehistoric society dominated by writing manipulators, themselves illiterate in our sense of the term, is the only approximate example I know of the technocratic danger that threatens us today. § But this is not a good example, and history can only teach us that it cannot teach us anything, since every historical situation is unique and incomparable, such as ours. We can only attempt to apprehend each situation as it is. Or, we must attempt to apprehend the new communication structures before they become fully autonomous from our Will. Therefore, in my opinion, we should not bang our heads against the wall of cybernetic programming and mass media, as this would be

a typically reactionary attitude. Or even
close our eyes before this wall and say that
this is all an exaggeration, since we can still
write, speak, sing, dance, and make love,
despite the communication revolution. But
we can no longer do these things as we did
them before, or, as the Egyptians did,
because before linear writing, they were
prehistoric, but today, we are no loger. We
should, in my opinion, attempt to actively
take control of the new structure of communication in favour of theoretical and
practical learning. However, I confess that I
do not know how to do that in practice.
I see several attempts of this around me,
but I am sceptical in relation to the results.
Nevertheless, it seems to me that the
dominance of aesthetic models, or in other
words, of that thing we called "art" before
the revolution, is where our greatest hope
of practically dominating the instruments
that threaten us lies. That is why my interest
is increasingly aimed at the critique of such
activities. § On the other hand, I believe
I do know how to take control of these
new instruments, through theory. That

is why I offered this course of lectures.
I am convinced that we must face such
instruments head-on, and from all sides, in
order to analyse them with every attention,
disposable methods, and calculations that
we are still capable of in relation to them.
This is not much, but is already something.
So that if we observe them critically, and
step back, then later, we will be able to leap
over them better, as long as we have not been
dominated yet. At least, this is the minimum
we can do so that we are not changed against
our will, but as we want to. *

METAFLUX // VILÉM FLUSSER

INTO IMMATERIAL CULTURE

THE SURPRISING PHENOMENON OF
HUMAN COMMUNICATION

GROUNDLESS

ARTFORUM // ESSAYS

MUTATION IN HUMAN RELATIONS

IN PRAISE OF SUPERFICIALITY

BEING JEWISH

BRAZIL // IN SEARCH OF THE NEW MAN

This book was composed by
Chagrin with Montserrat and
Jenson Recut fonts.

© Metflux Publishing 2016

www.metafluxpublishing.com

ISBN 978 0 9933272 5 4

CPSIA information can be obtained
at www.ICGtesting.com
Printed in the USA
LVOW04s0846220316

480111LV00069B/973/P

9 780993 327254

METAFLUX // VILÉM FLUSSER

§ The philosopher Vilém Flusser was born in Prague
in 1920 but emigrated to Brazil, fleeing from Nazi
persecution, at the outbreak of war in 1939, arriving
in Rio de Janeiro at the end of 1940, with his wife
and parents-in-law, after a short stay in London. The
Flussers settled in São Paulo during the 1940s, where
they lived for thirty two years. In the early years of the
1970s they moved back to Europe, settling first in Italy,
and subsequently in Robion, France, where they lived
until Vilém Flusser's untimely death in 1991 after a
car crash, as he left Prague at the end of a symposium.
§ During the years he lived in Brazil, Flusser wrote for
several Brazilian periodicals and taught at different
academic institutions, among them, the University of
São Paulo, the Brazilian Institute of Philosophy, and
the Institute of Technology and Aeronautics. His first
two books, *Lingua e Realidade* and *A História do Diabo*, were
published in Brazil during the 1960s. In the late 1970s,
and throughout the 1980s, Flusser travelled most of
Europe lecturing and participating in conferences and
symposia, during which time he published his most
well-known titles. He came to prominence in the field
of Media Philosophy after publishing his seminal book
Towards a Philosophy of Photography in 1984, shortly followed
by *Ins Universum der Technischen Bilder* in 1985, and *Die Schrift.
Hat Schreiben Zukunft?* in 1987. § As a polyglot, Flusser
wrote in four different languages, German, Portuguese,
English, and French. The Metaflux // Vilém Flusser
collection aims to present to an international readership,
high quality translations of Flusser's Brazilian writings,
including courses, monographs, essays, and letters, as
well as works originally written in English by the author.
§ The Metaflux // Vilém Flusser collection is possible
due to the generous support of Miguel Gustavo Flusser.